RETHINKING GOODNESS

SUNY Series in Ethical Theory

Robert B. Louden, Editor

RETHINKING GOODNESS

Michael A. Wallach
and
Lise Wallach

STATE UNIVERSITY OF NEW YORK PRESS

Published by
State University of New York Press, Albany

© 1990 State University of New York

All rights reserved

Printed in the United States of America

No part of this book may be used or reproduced
in any manner whatsoever without written permission
except in the case of brief quotations embodied in
critical articles and reviews.

For information, address State University of New York
Press, State University Plaza, Albany, N.Y., 12246

Library of Congress Cataloging-in-Publication Data
Wallach, Michael A.
  Rethinking goodness / Michael A. Wallach and Lise Wallach.
    p. cm. — (SUNY series in ethical theory)
  Includes bibliographical references.
  ISBN 0-7914-0299-1. — ISBN 0-7914-0300-9 (pbk.)
  1. Good and evil. 2. Liberty. 3. Conformity. 4. Autonomy
(Philosophy) 5. Individualism. 6. Common good. I. Wallach, Lise.
II. Title. III. Series.
BJ1401.W28 1990
170—dc20   89-21570
                                                                                     CIP

10 9 8 7 6 5 4 3 2 1

CONTENTS

Preface vii

1. **The Minimalist Predicament** 1
   - The Legacy of Liberalism
   - Calls to Abridge Autonomy
   - Another Way

2. **Student Voices on Values** 17
   - Work and Effort
   - Pairing Off
   - Living in Society

3. **Virtue Desired** 39
   - Greece before Plato and Aristotle
   - Plato and Aristotle
   - Buddha and Confucius

4. **The Mystification of Goodness** 53
   - The Good as God's Commands
   - The Severing of Virtue from Human Desire
   - The Philosophers

5. **What the Humanists Forgot** 69
   - The Good in Our Genes
   - The Insufficiency of Spontaneous Goodness

6. **Dealing with Differences** 95
   - Respect and Relativism
   - Can Ethical Beliefs Be Justified?

7.	Some Thoughts for Feminists, Communitarians, and Moral Educators	117
	• Feminism	
	• Community	
	• Moral Education	
Notes		135
Index		151

PREFACE

This book emerged for us from a concern with our society's pendulum swings between a secular liberalism that seems to promote self-indulgence, and a reactive authoritarianism—sometimes implicit, sometimes explicit, sometimes religious, sometimes not—that asks people in effect to cede their personal autonomy for the sake of larger societal goals. On the one hand is the typical liberal and secular humanist outlook that links tolerance and respect for differences with asking little ethically of others (and of ourselves): what might be termed ethical minimalism. We are not to infringe on others' rights, we are to respect their values and opinions—but apart from this, ethics is a matter of personal feelings. Going by one's feelings and allowing others to do the same preserves the autonomy of the individual, and this autonomy is held sacrosanct. Keeping ethics minimal is understood to be the only way of supporting what liberalism achieved.

On the other hand are those who decry the slide into self-centeredness and the preoccupation with becoming one's own person that seem to characterize much of modern American life. Recent examples range from the book by Robert Bellah and his collaborators, *Habits of the Heart*, to Carol Gilligan's *In a Different Voice*, to Alasdair MacIntyre's *After Virtue*, to Allan Bloom's *The Closing of the American Mind*. Each in its way is in part a reaction to the moral minimalism of our time. Each in its way urges mitigation of self-focus. But, as we will discuss, the solutions that they and others propose—some religious, some secular—each in its way sacrifices and circumscribes the autonomy of the individual.

Invocations of authority may be more blatant—as in the case of Allan Bloom, who seems eager to roll back modernity in the interests of order, derides complaints about domination, calling it merely a "buzzword," and sees in sexism and elitism reflections of the state of nature. Or invocations of authority may remain more implicit—as in the appeals in *Habits of the Heart* to the tradition of civic republicanism as a basis for renewed social and community concern, or in *After Virtue* to the claimed necessity of grounding ethics ultimately in the practices of a given tradition. We may be urged to limit the dominion of the principle of autonomy in the interests of furthering connection and care, as in the case of Carol Gilligan. Though they do it in different ways, all these responses to individualism or narcissism share the property of serving in effect to threaten autonomy. The predictable liberal reaction, then, as the threats to autonomy mount, is renewed insistence that ethics be left to each of us as a personal matter: the pendulum swings back.

Confronted by this conundrum, ethics has come onto hard times in our society for anyone who can't accept a grounding in religion. Is the minimalist emasculation of ethics a necessary consequence if we are to preserve individual freedom and autonomy? Is the ceding of autonomy the necessary price of an ethics that goes beyond personal preferences? If the answer to these questions must be yes, we are trapped between liberal license and authoritarian calls to limit autonomy. The society is inexorably forced to choose between freedom and narcissism on the one hand, morality and coercion on the other. It is a debilitating choice, one that polarizes and inflames us, one that erodes the basis for social life.

This book elaborates an argument that the answer to both questions is no. We argue that there is a way out from having to choose between freedom at the price of narcissism and morality at the price of coercion. Minimalism, we claim, is a mistake born of the way in which ethics came to be psychologically understood, a way forged in religion and then maintained even by those who rejected a religious grounding for ethics. We describe the origins of this misunderstanding in a Judeo-Christian heritage which eventuated in the extruding of goodness from the catalogue of our own wants. Western religion severed the link found in classical Greece, among other cultures, between virtue and human desire. Goodness became what God, not we ourselves, wanted. Goodness became an external imposition.

We argue that the ramifications of this externalization of ethics extended considerably beyond Western religion, affecting modern secular thinking as well. Some secularists came to insist on the necessity of curtailing liberty because we must be "shaped" and "socialized" toward virtue by temporal forms of authority.

Other secularists—the modern variety of humanists—came to consider environmental constraints the problem instead of the solution, viewing our wants as for the best until other people deform and distort them in morality's cause. In these scenarios, either freedom becomes culpable, or ethics itself becomes culpable. In both cases, outside agencies keep the significance they gained in Western religion as the source of moral curbs, controls, and prescriptions—although in the one case those agencies are accepted for the sake of making us good, and in the other they are rejected as enslaving us and making us ill. In both cases, autonomy and substantial ethics are cast thereby as opposites.

For reasons biological, psychological, and phenomenological, we claim this oppositional casting to be fundamentally in error. To see more than a minimal ethic as autonomy's converse rests on confounding thinking for oneself with favoring the personal—doing one's own thinking with thinking *of* oneself. It is because of this confusion, in our opinion, that minimalism in ethics—going by personal preferences and feelings—came to seem necessary for achieving and preserving autonomy. Once free of the confusion, however, we can achieve a non-authoritarian grounding for an ethics of strong social concern and commitment, a grounding that avoids the narcissistic problems of current liberalism and humanism without sacrificing their values of tolerance and liberty. The outside world can affect us ethically in ways consistent with our autonomy rather than opposed to it; but the culture seems to have lost touch with those ways. Understanding why—and recapturing and documenting the availability of these ways—is the business of this book.

Such an undertaking requires, in our view, a type of inquiry transcending the bounds within which ethics is usually studied— that of philosophy or religion. The inquiry needs to be interdisciplinary, in the sense of asking in as unbounded a way as possible how our terms of interpretation for ethics have come to be what they are. We have to look at the development of these terms of interpretation across time, consulting different fields of specialized knowledge as they are appropriate to the task. The danger, of course, is error; that is one reason why scholars specialize in the first place. But when the questions you are asking refuse to stay put obediently within one or another field, but keep migrating across them, the choice becomes either to give up on the questions or to hold tight to one's scholarly hat and follow them wherever they lead. Foolishly or not, we chose the latter path.

We had help and support in taking this route. The scholarly community functioned in an exemplary manner as our work unfolded and we sought counsel from other scholars, especially ones outside our home discipline of psychology. In the end, we have been the beneficiaries of much time and energy graciously devoted to reading and commenting on earlier drafts of all or parts of our material by scholars with particular expertise in classics, religion, philosophy, evolutionary biology, sociology, and psychiatry, as well as psychology. We are grateful for comments from Kurt Back, Robert Drake, Carl Erickson, David Falk, Joel Farber, Stanley Hauerwas, Richard Rorty, Jay Rosenberg, Geoff Sayre McCord, Keith Stanley, Paul Vitz, Mary Woolsey, and the publisher's reviewers. We also thank Martin Lakin and Naomi Quinn for helpful suggestions.

The students whom we interviewed were a source of inspiration to us in the seriousness with which they undertook their task. Finally, we thank Verble Roberts for transcribing the interviews and Pat Eichman for typing the manuscript. Both were highly competent and wonderfully cheerful.

1

The Minimalist Predicament

There is a crisis in our ethics. For many, ethics means no more than that we are not to infringe on the rights of others, and that we are to respect their values and opinions. Beyond this, we essentially should go by our own feelings. Perhaps we should be up front about what they are, but that is the extent of our obligations. This adds up to a minimal ethic; yet for many it seems the only possibility. After all, autonomy is important, and autonomy not only for oneself but for others. There is a need, therefore, to be tolerant toward people whose values differ from our own. Ethics becomes a shrunken arena; for the most part, only a personal matter. But limiting oneself to personal preferences hardly seems ethics at all. Personal preferences may readily change or lose all force. Is this ethics?

It is the triumph of liberalism, and no mean accomplishment. It is the response to rules and prescriptions that amounted to one person's oppressing or exploiting another. What liberalism accomplished, the humanist scholar Isaiah Berlin tells us, was "to seek to curb interference, exploitation, enslavement by men whose ends are theirs, not one's own." [1] The answer to authoritarian imposition, Berlin says, is "a situation in which as many individuals as possible can realize as many of their ends as possible, without assessment of the value of these ends as such, save insofar as they may frustrate the purposes of others." [2] Berlin is arguing in effect that the achievement of not allowing one person to dictate to another requires that all non-infringing ends have to be viewed as equally valid—an ethic of personal preferences. This book will affirm the premise but reject the conclusion. Concern for autonomy, we will argue, does not require minimalist ethics. The belief that it does springs from some mistaken turns made in the history of Western thinking.

Proponents of minimalist ethics do not always fully live that way but may catch themselves, apologetically, going beyond them. "'I do go around saying he shouldn't have done that or something like that, but when you come down to it, unless I'm in that other person's head I don't have the right to condemn them or anything like that.'" [3] Although you may lapse into doing it, any attempt to argue with others about ethics is unjustified. It is arbitrary imposition. All you can justifiably expect of others is that they go along with their convictions.

At other times, the minimalist wholeheartedly accepts the implication of moral solipsism, using this as a rationale for self-indulgent goals. A university president decries how higher education has changed from encouraging students to find and take up callings, to an arena for the seeking of personal advancement. "We seem to be turning out people who are bent on exploiting careers for their own ends rather than upon service through their professions for the sake of society." [4] If, apart from infringements on others, one end is as good as another, with subjective feelings the only arbiter, why not be out for oneself? Acting in line with what you want for yourself, disparaging moral compulsions as forms of moralizing, becomes a defensible, even courageous, pursuit. Looking back from the perspective of *Portnoy's Complaint, My Life as a Man,* or *The Professor of Desire,* at his youthful first novel, *Letting Go,* Philip Roth finds it, in its emphasis on duty and loyalty, to be obligation-ridden, overly solemn, fastidious. "Roth ... has often expressed impatience with the novel, declaring it in various interviews 'a devoted effort at self-removal and self-obliteration' and a work excessively preoccupied with 'conscience, responsibility, and rectitude.'" [5]

We are talking of ideals, then, and saying that our ideals themselves often push for a minimal ethic. It is not a question of aspiring to more and falling short. It is a question of the aspirations we do have, the aims we affirm. Perhaps this is not surprising when you consider the small amount of encouragement presumed experts offer for going beyond a minimal ethic. A respected textbook on career counseling lists the values of honesty, morality, and social welfare as on a par with money, physical appearance, and travel, among others. The book tells its readers,

"There are no right and wrong values in a free society. Values derive from the way an individual has been taught." [6] More generally, much that is offered by the modern social sciences to explain us to ourselves tends to justify the liberal world-view of letting people pursue their personal ends, whatever these may be.

The Legacy of Liberalism

Take psychology as an influential case in point. A broad range of psychology, both in its academic teachings about human motivation and in the forms of therapy it provides, has been found to favor attention to self as the first order of therapeutic business and individualism as an accurate account of our real concerns. [7] For example, the clinical psychologist Carl Rogers, who, according to a recent survey, "heads by far the list of those who have the greatest influence on counseling and psychotherapy," [8] writes on marriage that "a relationship between a man and a woman is significant, and worth trying to preserve, only when it is an enhancing, growing experience for each person." [9] No danger here of an obligation-ridden spouse. Commitment to the partner in your role of married person, rather than to your own growth, your own actualization, will hide you from yourself.

And while Freud may have been puritanical in comparison with Rogers, psychoanalytic theory has always understood neurosis as arising from insufficient gratification of feelings or impulses. Heinz Kohut, increasingly prominent these days in psychoanalytic circles, seemed if anything to be downplaying that puritanical strain and moving closer to a Rogerian acceptance of self-enjoyment. As an expositor of Kohut explains, the patient's "archaic or 'selfish' demands ... are not to be condemned (that is, the patient is not to be admonished to inhibit selfishness), but rather such demands are to be welcomed and understood as the expression of the self's drive to complete its development." [10]

The crown of that development, in turn, is understood in various academic formulations—an example would be Jane Loevinger's influential model of "ego development"—as something like autonomy, individuality, or self-fulfillment, which are seen as closely related. [11] Minimal ethics emerges as the very goal of such development: pursuit of individual preferences, respect for the autonomy of others.

Not only psychology among the social sciences is found to be individualistic and self-oriented. Another illustration would be economics. (To be sure, psychology has not given it much of an argument.) "Economists have from time to time inquired at the psychology shop for premises of behavior richer than greed, but have found none to their liking." [12] But economists have, for the most part, been quite content without invoking psychology to accept the sufficiency of self-interest as their premise for economic behavior. This is neoclassical methodology—"the dominant one in the English-speaking world." [13] As the social thinker Amitai Etzioni has noted, even attempts to accommodate seemingly unselfish forms of economic behavior typically keep the neoclassical assumption that self-interest is still operating in one form or another. [14] Once again, a minimal ethic becomes the corollary of such an outlook: not to interfere with others going by their own feelings, just as we go by ours.

In what is known of human history, minimalism as an ethical aspiration is a relatively new phenomenon. There have, of course, always been problems of people conducting themselves in ways that seemed wrong to somebody. Until the modern period, however, typical understandings on how you *ought* to conduct yourself—the reigning ideals—always were different from mere non-infringement. There would be roles and functions to carry out, contributions of various kinds to be made for the sake of what is outside the self—family, community defined more narrowly or broadly.

These were not even matters of explicit morality. Traditions and long-established lines of authority simply made extensive and widely accepted prescriptions concerning how to live. You had certain roles in life and these were defined in relation to the community of which you were a part. There was little notion of a separate individual. Your roles were sources of meaning to you—not masks that concealed you. Fulfilling your roles was playing your part in the order of things, as defined by custom, law, or superior beings both human and divine. The sociologist Peter Berger captures the retreat to the self that took place in the transition to modernity by noting that the concept of honor was replaced by the concept of dignity. "In a world of honor, the individual discovers his true identity in his roles, and to turn away from the roles is to turn away from himself .... In a world of dignity, the individual can only discover his true identity by emancipating himself from his socially imposed roles." [15]

Roles can, of course, be impositions. The existing regulations and arrangements of a society may be grossly oppressive and damaging. This is the lesson that the educated Westerner learned like no other, concluding that what really matters is the self you reach when roles are stripped away. If this is human reality, interference with the autonomy of that self becomes the hallmark of evil, or at least of mental illness; and good—or at least what is healthy—becomes the vague category of letting individuals "be themselves." As another social thinker describes this erosion in the significance of life outside the self, "social bonds and social engagement have receded in the face of inquiry about 'what am I feeling?'" [16]

Personal wants emerged as an explicit focus, never before given such clarity, and indeed often before given no attention at all. Lost in this process was something that may have been easier to grasp when the issue of what you want for yourself remained implicit: what we in fact most want—"for ourselves"—may sometimes, though not always, coincide with contributing to goals beyond the self. And many of these goals are advanced by our having functions in various kinds of communities—by our taking on the very roles now seen in the liberal vision as impositions and oppressive masks. To attend to such roles and functions *may* be to give up autonomy and submit to authority, but it also may be to pursue aims that though not without conflict are nevertheless our own.

The respect for individual self-consciousness that comprises the modern Western sensibility was bought at the price, then, of considering personal feelings to be what is most real. This had consequences not just for ethics, of course. Take the arts. The same retreat to the self is what the modern dancer Michael Ballard criticizes when he describes dancers who are doing what he considers aesthetically poor dancing. "They cannot trust themselves to find out what the movement demands rather than what their attitude about themselves demands. So they dance their attitude about themselves rather than dealing with the material." [17] And it is what the architecture critic Ada Louise Huxtable finds fault with when she describes postmodernism as ignoring architecture's traditional role of serving collective purposes or needs. Like Ballard's concept of bad dancing, such architecture becomes a kind of posturing—the architect's striking of poses. "With the renunciation of traditional social responsibilities as beyond his capacities or control, the architect has finally been freed to pursue style exclusively and openly." As a result, what gets done in the name of design becomes "an increasingly hermetic and narcissistic process." [18]

But it is implications for ethics that will concern us in this book. Can there be more than a minimal ethic without sacrificing what liberalism achieved? What grounds can be given for seeking more than that individuals each should have the right to go by their feelings, to find and follow their personal preferences? The problems with such an ethic have been receiving increasing attention these days. A psychotherapist, for example, when asked to consider what therapy does for the larger community, doubts that it contributes to the common good. "'The only community I ever think I'm adding to is the one of people who have been in therapy and talk like psychologists, you know, and that's not particularly positive.'" [19] Two main ways of coming to grips with these problems have been proposed. Both strike us as insufficient—as in fact supporting an authoritarian backlash that will in turn engender its own backlash. We will argue that a third direction of response is possible, however; one which breaks the cycles or pendulum swings between liberalism and authoritarianism, with a different type of solution.

Calls to Abridge Autonomy

The first direction of response to the minimalist predicament is a return to religion. Sociologist of religion Robert Bellah and his colleagues write, "A church that can be counted on and that can count on its members can be a great source of strength in reconstituting the social basis of our society." [20] They believe that the church idea shows people an authority in which they can participate rather than one which is imposed on them from outside. In this way, community can be rediscovered without having to give up individuality. Those for whom religion offers an acceptable source of authority can indeed use it as a basis for going beyond a minimal ethic. Taken seriously, the commandments to love God and to love your neighbor certainly can turn you away from personal concerns—although, of course, they also can be invoked as covers for the personal, as in doing good to get into heaven.

But for many, a religious route is unavailable. Proposing religion to them as a solution begs the question. It cannot be used precisely because they are skeptical of its claims to authority. They see their individuality as compromised within it. They are asked to join a community that practices submission to God's will. A religion like Christianity can involve conceptions of the supernatural for which they find no warrant. Notions about in-groups and out-groups, who is saved or chosen and who is not, are part of some religions and can be found repugnant. In any case, the bottom line often will be that one or another belief must be taken on faith—the very requirement that flies in the face of individual autonomy and gave rise historically to liberalism's circumscribing the hegemony of religious authority. After all, the Christian theologian Stanley Hauerwas acknowledges what Robert Bellah and his associates would seem to deny: that Christianity takes the idea "that we can and should be morally autonomous" to be a prideful pretension. [21]

The other direction of response to the problems generated by minimalism in people's ethics has been a secular one. At the extreme, liberalism is blatantly rejected and renewed authority is called for. The political philosopher Allan Bloom, fed up with the narcissistic excesses of contemporary American college students, chastises them in his recent best-seller for their preoccupation with avoiding exploitation and domination by others and their consequent focus on treating all as "persons," as equivalently free agents. Authorities have to take it upon themselves to impose standards. "It is childishness to say, as some do, that everyone must be allowed to develop freely." [22]

Many more moderate scholars are urging a resetting of the American balance more toward the side of the group and communion, feeling that it now is positioned too far toward the side of the individual and autonomy. Autonomy is no longer to be viewed as the virtue it once was, says Jerome Kagan, a prominent psychologist of child development. Earlier in our history, "autonomy became more virtuous." But now, "the balance between self-enhancement and communion has been lost, and the point of tension must be reset in order to restrain complete commitment to self-aggrandizement." [23]

We are to give up some of our autonomy in the interests of communion and kindness. The President of the American Psychological Association, in her 1985 Presidential Address, seeing "the sense of self or agency and the sense of selflessness or communion" as "contradictory impulses,"[24] decries the dominant focus on the personal and urges the undertaking of commitments to the smaller and larger communities we live in. An influential current psychological account of morality sees responsiveness to others as society's somehow acting on the individual in contrast to self-determination, and wants both in our morality.[25] By such terms of understanding, however, responsiveness to others becomes a mitigation of self-determination. An influential critique of individualist assumptions in descriptions of optimal morality wants the "view of the individual as socially embedded rather than as autonomous and self-centered" to receive more emphasis.[26] Carol Gilligan, a prominent feminist psychologist, arguing that women "arrive at an understanding of life that reflects the limits of autonomy and control," believes there is a more "feminine" principle of care and concern for others that should receive equal play in morality with the more "masculine" principle of autonomy.[27] Again and again in these forms of thinking, autonomy is pitted against communion or altruism, and concern for altruism or communion is understood as requiring diminution of autonomy.

But to see autonomy and concern for others as opposed in this way seems a fundamental error, one which undercuts the very attempts made by these social scientists to support altruism and commitment to others. For the liberal insight into the crucial significance of deciding for oneself—autonomy—is confounded thereby with advancing the interests of the self rather than the interests of others. Self-determination is confounded with self-advancement. As the costs of individualism become intolerable, the recommendation then comes in that more attention be given to sacrificing for others, "at least until the balance is restored."[28] But if autonomy really coincides with self-advancement, this is asking that autonomy be sacrificed—precisely the danger, of submission to someone else's authority, that liberalism wants to guard us against. Autonomy is allowed to stand as a justification for self-focus. Concern for others, for the welfare of the communities in which one participates, becomes, ironically enough, cheapened in this way even by those who want to urge it. For they are urging something seemingly opposed to autonomy, and therefore an imposition, or at least something less important or less valid since it involves the questionable comforts of conformity and submission.

Responsiveness to others, concern for their welfare, contributions to larger social units: such goals seem demeaned if they are understood as entailing the sacrifice of autonomy or self-determination. They then can only be lesser goals, perhaps needed for preserving the global commons, but at best a celebration of passivity, yielding, surrender—the security that comes from immersion in the group. They become values for the weak, not values of choice. Communitarian goals then depend on the use of external forces, increasing the temptation to apply them. Liberals have heard this song before. An authority—now perhaps a secular social science expert—is aborting freedom and encouraging self-abnegation in the name of "character." Sooner or later, the use of superior power is recommended to engineer the desired outcome. "Acts of honesty, cooperation, and nurturance are public events that the staff of a school can tally and use to assign individual evaluations that are understood to be essential complements to subject mastery."[29] Ethics earns you points. Looking moral becomes a way of making it—rising in the bureaucracy of a totalitarian state's party, for example.

The pendulum swings back, then, to an increased use of social constraints and pressures. Some use, of course, must always be made of them, as a warrant against people's infringing on the basic rights of others. But they hardly provide an inspiring rationale even for minimal ethics, much less for anything else. At best, they encourage the image of behaving ethically, not the reality. I should seem honest, cooperative, and nurturant of others, for example. Whether I *really* am humble, compassionate, caring, and so on, does not matter, as long as I keep up appearances. Indeed, deception may be to my advantage. Further, if I behave in certain ways because of social sanctions, that cannot really be something I take pride in. It is not behaving autonomously—it is acting on the basis of something imposed from without.

What about conscience? Can conscience provide us with a satisfactory rationale for going beyond minimalism—a basis for choosing autonomously not only to seem, but to be, concerned about other people and matters that go beyond the self? Perhaps yes, if we can understand conscience as our own best voice, as reminding us of what we ourselves most want. This is not, however, the view of conscience held by many skeptical cosmopolitans of today, especially if they have been influenced by the concepts of modern social science. Here, conscience is seen as an effect of norms and constraints internalized from the society. We feel good about ourselves when we act in ways that are approved of; we feel guilt or shame when we do things that the society defines as wrong. The process at work is socialization. The self-esteem or guilt means we are now administering to ourselves the approvals and disapprovals, rewards and punishments, that previously have been meted out to us by "agents of socialization." To say they have socialized us is to say the approvals and disapprovals have become self-administering. Like prison trusties, we are doing the work of the authorities for them. As a recent article expresses the psychological consensus on this, "Virtually all the explanations of altruism have assumed that it is a socialized behavior." [30]

But then conscience, too, fails to offer a satisfactory basis for our autonomously choosing to behave ethically. If the reason we should not cheat is so as not to feel guilty, and guilt is merely the residue of external impositions by agents of socialization, then our reason for not cheating has little validity. It may make more sense, when faced with temptations to cheat, for us to talk ourselves out of feeling guilty rather than for us to avoid cheating. Conscience becomes a form of weakness. Tempering ourselves to cheat without feeling guilt becomes a sign of strength.

This may well be the current situation for many people, in fact, considering the growing acceptance of lying—for example, on income tax returns and on resumés. A journalist lamenting this trend points out, "Traditionally, the checking force against the use of deception was guilt. The man accused of lying lost not only his clean record but, often, his self-esteem." [31] The danger is that now lying no longer entails loss of self-esteem. On the contrary, lying is often viewed as justified for self-advancement, with that as what self-esteem depends on. The suggested answer is a return to the traditional checking force. Authorities must shore up the arrangements that tie lying to guilt or shame. In other words, more impositions again. An independent thinker may well smell a con here, and conclude that self-esteem really accrues to those who beat the system.

Both the religious and the secular responses to the minimalist predicament support authoritarian solutions in the sense of weakening the self-determination or autonomy that forms the bedrock of liberalism. Apart from obeying the dictates of religious or secular forms of authority, are we left with an equivalence of ends, infringements on others excepted? Is ceding autonomy—one's own and respect for that of others—the necessary price of going beyond a minimal ethic? If so, many, including many who are most educated and sophisticated, will balk at paying it. Whatever its attractions, authoritarianism can only produce a liberal counterreaction, and then the problems of minimalism all over again.

Another Way

We have suggested the outlines of another possibility, however, in arguing that autonomy and self-focus are not the same. This book will claim that the core of the minimalist predicament lies in confounding the two, eclipsing thereby the *non*impositional meanings the environment can have. Self-determination does not limit us to an ethic of personal preferences, because self-determination is different from spontaneous self-expression or advancing one's personal interests. Deciding for oneself is different from deciding in favor of oneself.

Deciding for oneself can be quite consistent with putting the interests of others ahead of one's own. This is what, in all deliberation, you may decide you most want and care about. But it indeed may *take* deliberation and also sometimes reminders and arguments from others to recognize these wants. What I most want need not be what I first think I want. I may choose to forego personal ends because, in my own best, most thoughtful judgment, other considerations take precedence.

A parent may sacrifice personal consumption in favor of deciding to pay for a child's education. A legal adjudication may go against one's personal advantage and yet be accepted willingly, even if unhappily, because one believes in the importance of the legal system on which it rests. These are wants, but not based on personal fulfillment or arbitrary feeling. They may in fact go against one's immediate feelings and preferences. Nor are they merely based on long-term or "enlightened" calculations of self-interest. You really want that child to flourish, whether or not this serves to benefit you in your old age. You really want to see the kind of community life made possible by the rule of law, whether or not your own status or income will be affected in the long run. They are what you think is the right thing to do even if personally disadvantageous or unfulfilling. And not just what is "right for you," but quite generally. You can defend these wants of yours with reasons that you feel would hold for anyone.

The constraints established by roles and obligations, by commitments, by rules, may help you to act upon and to accomplish what, upon consideration, you most want. There is no reason to identify your most deeply held wants with those that are easiest to sense or grasp or enact. This is perhaps more apparent when thinking about learning a skill, where you accept instruction and, temptations to the contrary notwithstanding, commit yourself to training and practicing—kinds of compliance that can be motivated nevertheless by your own wish to become a dancer or a musician or a swimmer. The idea of doing this might, of course, be someone else's, not yours, but it can be yours. And if yours, willingness to follow a teacher's prescriptions might be motivated by the enlightened self-interest of wanting to excel, to lord it over others, to be lionized—but your willingness can also, or instead, be motivated by your caring about the dance form, about a kind of music, about the sport. You want to do what it calls for.

So, too, with the commitments of friendship, of parenthood, of marriage, of membership in a group, of citizenship, where taking on responsibilities can foster the well-being of others or of a social order you believe is a good thing. Again, these may be matters of duress, whether of explicit kinds or the more covert impositions of socialization, but need not be. And if willingly undertaken, kindness or loyalty or keeping one's word or doing one's part in the group may matter to one in its own right, not just as the conclusion of a calculus of self-interest. Yet coming to identify these as my wants may take reflection, examination, discussion. Compliance with roles or expectations may be motivated by my own genuine desires. This is different from submissive conformity to what I do not really want. And I retain the responsibility of having to distinguish between the two, difficult though it may be.

It is not easy for people to see such things these days in our society. This is a book about why. A chronicle of that difficulty is the Pilgrim's Progress shown by Will Barrett in Walker Percy's *The Last Gentleman*. [32] Locked within himself, "eyeballs rolled up in his eyebrows," [33] dreamlike in his drifting spontaneity, Barrett recoils from the still more extreme alienation of his fiancee's brother, Sutter Vaught, a decadent and despondent womanizer whose cynicism is complete. Barrett is gingerly getting hold of the satisfaction that comes from making and keeping commitments to others—meeting obligations to his fiancee, having a family, contributing to a community. But he respects Sutter, and Sutter mocks Barrett's intentions as phony and conformist, a selling out.

Barrett, afraid Sutter will kill himself, renews Sutter by loving him, by showing him that he needs Sutter. Barrett learns, and tries to teach Sutter, that taking such responsibility for another is not enslavement but the beginning of freedom.

The death of any but a minimal ethic after liberalism's arrival on the scene was inevitable because of the way morality had come to be—and still mostly is—understood. It tends to be viewed as distinct from human desire or motivation and therefore necessarily impositional. It is a "should," something we are "supposed to do," not something we want to do. Religion, having established the warrant for human morality as residing in God, became suspect to many Westerners for its requirement of faith and ultimate unamenability to further justification. Ethics having been banished to a divine source beyond us, skepticism about that source then brought ethics into question. Our own inclinations, it was assumed, could not be moral without God. Indeed, the function of morality was to curb those very inclinations—to make us go against them. The death of God meant the death of any but a minimal ethic as well, because it had become inconceivable that we could want to be moral on our own. Perhaps, however, we can and do.

Which is not to suggest that whatever we want will be in line with the good. The point is not to reinvent Rousseau and, in the manner of Carl Rogers and many other psychotherapists, find good in spontaneity and indict the environment for constraining us. Our spontaneous feelings may differ from, and need to be tamed by, other considerations which are no less our own desires for being difficult to recognize or act on. For freedom does not mean ease; our immediate preferences can be just as enslaving as the impositions of others. Some of our wants themselves may be "ethical"—aimed as such at benefitting others, at fulfilling responsibilities, at maintaining commitments—rather than selfish. But that is very different from claiming that asserting our personal wants and resisting all constraints must be good. It can take discipline to achieve what we most want, and even to find out what that is. And the effect of the environment can be to clarify rather than confuse us about and inhibit those wants.

Morality under liberalism dropped out with God, to be reinstated for liberals only in the romantic and illusory form that identified it with being true to our own feelings and personal preferences. Since these, of course, can be fickle or lose their compellingness, little of morality remains. When the problems caused by minimalism then mount, the responses tend to call for abridgement of autonomy, supporting renewed imposition, secular if not religious. Or the problems are denied or finessed in the name of autonomy and tolerance. Yet the problems are real, as a society with little sense of community or common purposes, and much alienation, cynicism, and pursuit of the personal, testifies. The importance of autonomy, on the other hand—of making one's own decisions—is real also.

The conception of morality as something quite separate from desire is, in fact, a comparatively recent development in the history of thinking about such matters. Morality as "shoulds" that are utterly distinct from "wants" was not the view in earlier Western thinking, nor in other traditions. This book makes the case that severing the tie between morality and our own wants or desires was a mistake, but that it is equally a mistake to view our wants as for the best until other people deform them. Because some of our wants are not selfish, autonomy is consistent with more than a minimal ethic. Control by outside forces is not the only way to have an ethics that goes beyond individuals and their personal preferences. Because others of our wants *are* selfish, we have choices to make, conflicts to resolve, in which the issue is competing desires and wishes *of our own*, not the self versus pressures and "shoulds" from the environment. And it may be *either* the selfish *or* the unselfish wants that are immediately obvious to us, or that only become evident with "consciousness raising." Other people can help us discover and keep in mind what we ourselves care most about. They are not just sources of imposition or of the comforts of self-surrender.

The first order of business, undertaken in the next chapter, is to make clear the meaning of minimalism in people's lives. We do so by considering excerpts from interviews, focusing on examples that show minimalist groundings of conduct. The aim is to assemble, by means of real people's voices, a composite portrait of a type of person, all too frequent on the current scene; to consider the ramifications of an outlook. The voices are those of college students who were willing to talk about the ethical ideals they aspire to fulfill—what really matters to them about right and wrong, good and bad. Some of the properties of minimalism can become clearest through contrast with alternative outlooks. Minimalist narratives also, therefore, will be compared with ones that go beyond a minimal ethic.

Our intent in this next chapter is depictive. We are describing an ethical outlook that turns the very absence of moral demands into a presumptive virtue. It is an outlook that follows logically if autonomy is esteemed and if ethics is seen as deriving from something external to ourselves. Not to give primacy to personal goals is then to submit to control by outside agencies, covertly if not overtly applied. Going beyond minimalism in ethics is then to accept imposition. Those who do go beyond a minimal ethic while thinking of themselves as autonomous can on this view only be deceiving themselves. Their autonomy is a sham, the self-deception of a socialized conscience.

Then, in the chapters following, we consider what brought it about that ethics came to be so widely understood as an external imposition, apparently necessitating minimalism for achieving and preserving autonomy. We will argue that this view is a mistaken holdover from some earlier lines of thought in Western history. We will claim that a warrant can be supplied, without God and consistent with the autonomy of the individual, for much more, ethically, than merely abiding by personal preferences and mutual non-infringement. We will suggest that a different story can be told about ethics.

If the minimalists are wrong about what autonomy requires, the way would be open for them to reconsider whether minimalism is morally desirable. Unless it can sustain its claim to being the only means of honoring personal freedom, minimalism loses the high ground to which liberals assigned it. If a more substantial ethic is congruent with one's own autonomy and that of others, rather than necessarily impositional, those who live that way may be correct, rather than self-deceived, for believing their path freely chosen, if that is how it seems to them. Minimalists may in this way discover that they would rather be otherwise. And those whose ethics already are otherwise may find themselves less on the defensive against accusations of weakness or lack of self-knowledge.

2

Student Voices on Values

What we are concerned with here is not that ethical conduct frequently falls short of ethical ideals. Thus it has always been and always will be. What seems newsworthy, however, is that these days the ideals themselves often ask for little. Not much is aspired to ethically. The moral sphere is narrowly delimited. This chapter will illustrate what such ethical minimalism actually looks like, and the role that autonomy plays.

We invited upper-division college students at an elite national institution—Duke—to come and talk individually about what is important to them in the area of ethical ideals and values. We told them that, if they volunteered, they would be asked to describe what good and bad and right and wrong really mean to them, and that what they said would be recorded on tape for possible publication. Proceeding in open-ended fashion, we listened to what each student had to say about their values, and, where it seemed desirable, asked for clarification and illustrations.

Our speakers were thus articulate young people, at a point in their lives at which—through their recent contacts with different points of view and their soon-to-come entry into the "real world"—issues of values could be expected to have a particular salience. Their words should represent in especially vivid ways thoughts that are likely to be in the minds of others as well. We considered them to be in a good position to serve as what anthropologists would call "cultural informants."

Excerpts from what they said follow, such as seem particularly good examples of minimalism and its opposite. Through these we hope to make more clear the concrete meaning of minimalism, and how it is promoted by the prevalent view that our real desires are self-oriented and that the source of ethics lies outside ourselves. We hope to show in this chapter that it is on this view that the relation between minimalism and autonomy, treated as obvious by so many, hinges. If this view can be put aside as a misconception, the relation between minimalism and autonomy disappears. No ground then remains for thinking of minimalists as any more autonomous than non-minimalists.

(Irrelevant details in the narratives have been changed to preserve confidentiality.)

Work and Effort

Often, the most revealing indications of what people really care about concerning right and wrong turn out to be biography and autobiography: speakers commenting on their own lives and the lives of others. To describe the minimalist outlook will largely be to consider its concrete manifestations. These fell naturally into different broad categories of existence, which serve as the framework for what follows. The first of these is work and effort. In the service of what kinds of ends are work and effort to be undertaken? What makes them worthwhile—what justifies them?

> I have an obligation to myself—to do what makes me happy. That's why I'm putting myself through torture in going to this school for four years and then hopefully going to law school. Not really because I want to go to school because school doesn't thrill me, but because I know if I don't go to school, I'm not going to be able to do what I want, and if I don't do what I want, I'm not going to be happy. So that's an obligation to myself, and other than that, besides my family and boyfriend, I don't think I really have any obligations. I mean I guess I have an obligation to be a decent human being to the rest of society. I have no right to do anything that would hurt society, but beyond that—I mean, no one else feels they have an obligation and no one else does anything. I'm just not even going to waste my time any more with anyone or anything that doesn't have a certain value to me.
>
> I want to be successful. I want to be able to live like I would not have to worry about anything—not have to worry about

money, not have to worry about other people supporting me. I think about that a lot when I sit there and study and go, "Oh my God, I don't want to study for this test." I tell myself, "Yes, you *do* want to study for this test, because you want to get into law school and be a success." I just want it so bad. There's nothing else I want. I just wish I could tell them when I apply at law school, "Look, I just want this. This is my biggest goal in life. You could just kill me after I become a lawyer and I'd die happy."

The meaning of becoming a lawyer seems here almost entirely to be the extrinsic one of its affording status and independence. It is a way to make money, to not have to depend on anybody else. The speaker's primary sense of obligation seems to be directed toward attaining status and position. Personal ambition is the imperative that keeps her working. The use to which the law degree can be put seems so secondary to the status implied by possession of it that she can joke about dying happy once she gets it.

Here is another speaker for whom self-gain and independence seem paramount:

I don't have any idea whatsoever what I want to do when I get out of school.... There are some people around I guess that don't really care if they don't make money, but that's key to me. I've grown up never really wanting—you know, I never needed anything and I got a lot of things that I definitely didn't need but that I wanted—and I never can stop wanting. I always want more, want better.... I don't want to depend on another person—a man or anybody else—to give me my money because you can't depend on someone else always. You have to be ready to stick up for yourself—and to provide for yourself. I want to be able to have all sorts of wonderful things and so since I'm the person that has to do it, then I have to make a lot of money.

Centering on personal income, success, status, can bring in its wake a tolerance for dishonesty if those ends will be furthered thereby:

There's this friend of our family who's in real estate. I guess you could say he's incredibly hedonistic. He really likes to have a good time. He has an excellent sense of humor. He's very successful, very, very well-known, and he—it's sort of interesting—he bends the rules that he really doesn't think affect anybody. Like—I'll give you an example. There are these zoning regulations sometimes against building something he wants to set up, and he uses his connections to get exceptions and waivers. I don't lose respect for him for that. You know, who really loses? Does anybody really lose anything in that?

He really represents a lot of things that I want to be. He has a very strong personality. He's very well respected. He's very well off. He loves to have a good time. He loves to enjoy life. He loves to travel. He really—he knows how to have a good time and he's very, very stable, very self-founded, very sure of himself, very self-confident, and he seems to really have achieved happiness—and of course success too. If I could just get one of those I'd be happy, you know, so he really—he is probably the one person who idealizes everything I want.

There is no loss of respect for this friend when he is found to tamper with the law in the service of his own gain. If anything, the speaker seems all the more admiring of him for getting away with it. You respect others—and yourself—for obtaining the signifiers of success. Cutting legal corners toward that end is acceptable if you don't harm others directly, but hurting others indirectly through violating zoning regulations for personal profit is viewed as not really hurting anybody.

The self seems the focus in these ways of thinking about what you do. Your activities are self-aimed: to make money for yourself, enhance your position, enjoy yourself, increase your possessions, travel, have whatever comes with status. You are doing the work for the money or status, as a straightforward exchange that exhausts the significance of the activity. You expend effort for the gain it brings you. That is being autonomous, self-founded, doing what you want.

Alternatively, the world need not be viewed as your oyster, to be exploited for personal benefit. You can feel obligated to give to the world. You can feel that you owe it something. A major reason for work and effort may lie in what they can contribute to something outside the self. This sort of conception seems evident in the following speaker's weighing of competing ends:

I have an aunt—a great-aunt, really—who's over ninety and she raised me and everything. I feel obligated to spend as much time with her as possible because she's not doing very well. There's not too much time left and she means an awful lot to me. But I work a lot in the community. I work at a counseling center and I work as a child advocate for four neglected children. I'm a big sister for them basically. So I have responsibilities to them too and it's often a conflict, you know, of what I'm going to do.

My aunt has given me so much, I feel like I owe her my time. She gets so happy when I go and see her. She tells me the same stories over and over and I love to hear them. It's great. But I feel like I need to spend more time with my children because they're going to be coming up to court soon and it's going to be a question of re-establishing them someplace else. So that's a big conflict right now: which is more important—I mean how big an obligation do children have to their parents and those who raised them? And sometimes it's hard to figure out if you owe it to them or owe it to the children that are coming next—you know, is that how you can pay them off or something. I don't know. I'm still thinking about it.

The speaker just considered looks at herself as part of a generational series: helping the next generation is a way of paying her dues to those who raised her. The world makes competing claims on one's work and effort; viewing oneself as a recipient of benefits held in trust and to be passed along helps in deciding what to do. Are these senses of obligation just unhealthy encumbrances, to be resisted in the name of freedom? Can the only freely assumed obligations be ones owed the self? As the next speaker shows, other obligations needn't mean obliviousness to what you might want for yourself, but do mean dethroning the self from the position of sole contender:

The summer after my freshman year I was involved in a sales group. They were selling encyclopedias for children and we were going to be sent who knows where to sell these encyclopedias. A friend of mine had done it before and he had made a lot of money, and I needed money, so I thought it sounded good. So I went to the training and ended up getting placed in Atlanta, and everyone was real excited because we were going to make a lot of money there because they had so much, right? So we got there and we found out you learn a lot, right away. You learn that the people with the big houses—really huge houses—aren't the ones to approach because the maid will just slam the door in your face. Then that left the middle class homes and the very, very poor homes. . . .

There's the problem: the poor homes were the easiest to sell. They were pushovers. First of all because they wanted to move up, and second of all because—I don't know—they just weren't sophisticated enough to understand what you were doing. We had to memorize a speech; we had all kinds of ways to get in the door and to stay there. . . . I didn't feel really comfortable about the pushiness because that's not my nature at all, but you see all these people around you who have done it and have been successful and they don't seem like terribly bad people. So anyway I had all kinds of waverings the whole time I was doing it, but I was doing it anyway and part of it was the fact that I was going to, you know, make this money. . . .

I ended up getting out of it like one month into the summer. I was supposed to stay four months. What I learned from it was that I didn't make a strong enough decision on my own. I was too willing to be enticed by the money and not thinking enough about the fact that, "Hey, do these people really need these books, because you don't even know how good they are."

This speaker, needing money, takes a type of summer job where it looks like the income should be good: selling encyclopedias for children. It quickly becomes evident that the way to make money is to sell to the poor because they can be manipulated. Skeptical that these people's children really will be helped this way, the speaker quits despite the social pressure of being part of a sales group. For this speaker, personal goals are not the only priority. They are not to be pursued at the expense of considering what would be best for others. It looks, furthermore, as if the greater autonomy here is shown in going against, rather than focusing on, gains for the self. Can it only be a delusion to view leaving the sales group as an act of independence rather than of submission to an internalized sense of guilt? May it instead be those with minimal ethics who are deluded when they justify a narrow focus on personal benefit in terms of independence, having a strong personality, or sticking up for themselves?

Pairing Off

Characterizing the meaning of good and bad often led speakers to bring up issues concerning sex. For minimalists, obligations to the self again are the focus. Consider the following examples:

> There is a situation I know where the man and the woman have been married for like ten years—something like that—and they're really close. They really love each other, you know—they're friends. They come home and they talk and they have a drink, and they do everything that they can together, except for the man because he had a very sort of strict and rigid upbringing has had his whole life very bad attitudes about sex and as the marriage wore on, he just became less and less interested *period* in sex. And the woman, who hoped that this would change once they got married, her interest in sex hasn't lessened at all. So as a consequence she's been forced to live without it for years.
>
> And it happened that she met a man who is married—also, quote–unquote, "happily"—I'm not sure about his situation but from what she tells me—and they started sleeping together. And on the surface, this would seem like a breach of loyalty—I mean to her husband—because she's sort of sharing what's supposed to be the most intimate encounter, and what—one of the, you know, foundations of marriage is that you don't sleep with other people. But, she hasn't *told* him. Because she knows it would hurt him. But I think that a sexual need is a very basic thing, and I don't think that because this man has been warped in a way that maybe he can't help, that she should have to go along with his character deformation or deprivation. I don't think that's fair. And I don't think that divorce is a solution because every other aspect is something that they like and they've built a life together. So, you know, that's a case where adultery, so to speak—is a solution. It's a way of keeping the marriage together and of satisfying the person who isn't being satisfied by the relationship. . . .

> I think dishonesty is immoral. The one thing I believe is that—that lying is—and more subtle than lying—hypocrisy, all sorts of social hypocrisy, or people pretend that they like each other because they're so scared of having enemies when in actuality as soon as the person has gone they're cutting down everything the other person says. . . . I guess I think dishonesty is a basis of immorality. But then like look at this woman not telling her husband that she's sleeping with someone else. It's just—there's no catchall, you know.

Here is a second example:

> I have two serious boyfriends—one of two years, and one of eight months, and they don't really know about each other. And like my friends say to me, "Well, this is really wrong. I can't believe you're doing this, especially to your boyfriend of two years—that's just wrong." And I guess it is in a way, because I'm really—I could be hurting people if they would ever find out. They'd probably kill me. But still, I'm just doing what I think is right. I'm not going to get married, so why—why can't I just have—the one guy of two years doesn't—won't allow me to go out with other people. I have no choice. I either go out with him seriously or I don't go out with him at all. And I want to go out with him, so I have to lie to him. And the other—I don't know—it's just—just gotten into a serious relationship. I never started out to be like that, but anyway I'm just like lying every day, because I could be getting off the phone with one of them, you know, while the other one's walking in my door or something. But it's just what I—I feel. It's not right but it's right for me because I'm having a good time and I'm happy with it. . . .
>
> I don't like to lie. I was raised not to lie. That was one thing my mother used to—if my sisters and I were ever punished for anything it was for lying. So I don't lie unless I really have to . . . . This is a case where I have to because I want this—I want—it's just like with Harvard Business School. If I had to lie to everyone in this world to get into Harvard I would do it, because it's something *I* want, and I guess—I guess I'm just a selfish person, but I think I've worked too hard in my life not to have what I want.

A third student says:

> I've been seeing a man who's married.... A friend of mine told me she thought that I should get out of this relationship as soon as possible. I listened, you know, and I thought about it—but I decided I wasn't going to accept that because that's not what I—it's not what *my* values told *me*.
>
> ... A friend used to say I had a self-preservation instinct—you know, that I do whatever would make me happiest, whatever it happened to be—whether it matched some kind of value or not. I guess I don't really think of myself as having a stiff structure of values. I can change them or I can abandon them or create new ones. It seems kind of strange that—I always—when you were younger, you thought that values were something that, kind of like rules that you put down and that's how you lived your life. But I've never been able to find those rules so I finally gave up and said, "Forget it."
>
> So it depends I guess if you think you're—if you're happy with the person that you are, then you'll just go with your own judgments and hope that if you hurt someone they tell you. Or if you do something that *you're* not happy with, you'll figure it out. So it's not a *decision* per se, it's just kind of what happens. It's like I look back and say, "Sometimes you're selfish and sometimes you're not," rather than looking forward and saying, "Am I going to be selfish or not in this situation?"

The first of these speakers condones a situation where a married woman sleeps with a man other than her husband because it is only fair that this woman should be able to satisfy her sexual need, and her husband has problems about sex. Since it would hurt the husband to know, the wife doesn't tell him. Even though the speaker views dishonesty as a basis of immorality, this dishonesty is accepted. The couple, we are told, are really close—really love each other—but the possibility that the husband might want to try to change seems to be ignored. In any case, it simply is viewed as not fair to expect the wife to make a sexual sacrifice because of her love for her husband. The dishonesty that really seems wrong to the speaker is dishonesty about feelings. Other dishonesties are acceptable in the service of sexual feelings and acting to satisfy sexual desires.

The next speaker talks of not liking to lie. She only lies if she has to in order to get what she wants, but for that she is entitled, with perhaps some ambivalence, to do so. She lies to one serious boyfriend about also having another. The one boyfriend wouldn't keep seeing her if he knew about the other one. Therefore, in her view, she has no choice but to lie because her feelings tell her to go out with both—it is what makes her happy. She resists advice from friends not to lie this way. The obligation that matters is to be true to your feelings.

The same holds for the speaker who rejects her friend's advice to stop seeing a married man. She will continue seeing him because that is what makes her happiest. You go with what makes you happiest, and hope that if you hurt someone else in the process, they will let you know. Once again, you follow your own feelings.

For such speakers, identifying your feelings or needs tells you what you really want. Your feelings or needs seem to be thought of as in some sort of realm apart—as what is most important and real—with your highest duty being to attend to them, act on them, and resist forces that would deflect you from them—even though, ironically, this may itself look like a form of subjugation rather than the freedom and independence it is meant to be.

With commitment to the self as central, the upshot can be a profound suspicion and malaise over the possibility of an enduring commitment to a partner:

> Marriage kind of scares me off when I think about it, because I wonder if I'll ever—if I'll ever find someone that I'm going to want to stay with for my whole life.... So I don't know if—I don't know if people are supposed to be, if they were actually meant to be monogamous.

This speaker worries whether marriage is consistent with the commitment "to yourself and to be happy." Compare the next speaker, who thinks about marriage in much less self-referential terms:

> Marriage to me would be a commitment—literally a life-long commitment to another person, which is something—it's big—it's the biggest thing you can probably do in one's life. It

should be—it should be the neatest, most exciting thing—a real special thing. It's a once in a lifetime deal, getting married, because it's that much of an obligation—that big of a commitment—on a very large scale. And it's—I don't know, there's, see—I was going to say that it's—the whole idea—to me it's the whole idea of life comes out of all the love that you give and receive. That's the whole purpose, meaning of life. There's no more. It's not money or anything else. To me that's the whole idea.

Here, marriage has a meaning that takes you out of yourself and towards another. Trying to explain that meaning, trying to grapple with why the commitment made to the other person is so deeply significant, this speaker comes to the notion that the whole purpose of life is the giving and receiving of love.

Which is not to deny that faithfulness to a partner may be difficult. It is, however, found to be of value in its own right. It is seen as important—not just an impediment that gets in the way of what one wishes or feels. Commitment to the other is itself a real want. Here is what another speaker says about this:

Being faithful to the girlfriend is one thing I find very important—very difficult sometimes, especially around here .... She goes to another college.... And it's not—it's not as much the being away that makes it difficult, as—I mean that's part of it, that's obviously part of it—but just the fact that there are other people that you like a lot and that you'd like to spend time with, and that entails certain things, certain expectations on their part.... I think it's very important to me not to hurt her or worry her more than necessary, and that's part of the—the obligational part of a relationship instead of the companionship, which are probably equally important.

When commitment to the other member of an enduring partnership becomes recognized as a value, one's sexual needs or gratifications can seem less to the point. Not because they don't matter, but because to focus on them in isolation can distort their meaning. Consider the following speaker's changing views on sex:

Throughout high school we dated, you know, dated around like everybody else. And then I settled into a very established relationship.... I developed my own ideas as to what was sexually moral and everything.... I had this idea that if two people really love one another then it was all right. I didn't think that you needed a piece of paper saying, "Yes, we're married." As such, you know, the relationship got more serious and we did engage in intercourse for a small amount of time. Like for a while it was very often and then it slacked off a lot because I became very uncomfortable with it. I realized that I did love the person very much but it didn't—there was something that wasn't there. There was something that was missing and I was thinking, "Is this really right, because I don't feel right about it. I don't feel ashamed about it but it just doesn't feel like it should." And I don't think I was pushing unrealistic standards on it, it's just that I didn't feel comfortable in that situation. I didn't feel like we had known each other enough or we—we just hadn't shared enough or made it—I don't want to say "official," but that's the only word that's coming to mind.

She was a little bit more on the other side so that caused some problems.... She was like, "Well," you know, "we don't make love any more. We haven't—it's been months. What's the problem?" I was just like, "Why am I bothering—why should I care?" And she I think had always been able to—although she felt very intimate about it, she didn't feel like she had to absolutely know with that individual person that that's the person she was going to be with all that time.

And I just told her, "Look, it's not that I don't necessarily *want* to be, it's just I don't *know* yet, and if I don't *know*, then I just—it's not feeling the way it should emotionally."

And I've come to the decision that I think this is a good reason not to have premarital intercourse, at least from my standpoint, because with me I just didn't feel right then. I don't think that it was because it's just—it's "wrong," you know—I don't agree with that. And a couple of times I've talked to people, I've gotten the same kind of thing once I get over this barrier that, you know, "Oh sure, sex—no problem." It wasn't really everything that they had hoped it would be, and I—I think that could be a major reason why....

So I found out kind of quickly—kind of the hard way too, I think—but I found out that, at least for me, I don't think it's—

it's right because I don't think you are ready to handle it yet. Beforehand you're ready to handle a lot of other things, and even very deep emotional commitments, but I think, at least for me, that is something that is so—I don't know—precious, treasured, whatever. That's something that should be shared only by people who really know that, "Yes, we love one another and we want to spend the rest of our lives together."

Is it, again, merely succumbing to the impact of earlier socialization pressures that leads this speaker to stop his sexual activity? Is it the delayed workings of a guilty conscience, whereby his otherwise healthy acceptance of sexual gratification has become neurotically inhibited? That analysis would consider illusory his own reasons for changing his mind on premarital sex, or would treat them as rationalizations. May it not rather be the minimalists whose preoccupation with the self eventuates in a distorted appreciation of their real wants?

Living in Society

Minimalists are focused on their personal needs, on seeking their own gratification or advancement. To do other than that is to allow yourself to be imposed upon by external forces. This rendering of the requirements for autonomy tells you not only what to work for and what to do about sex. It also colors your manner of social living generally.

Society as a framework has little separate positive meaning for minimalists. The arrangements it signifies, or can signify, define nothing to support or further apart from benefits to you. Social life is a tool, an instrument. Wresting whatever benefits from it you can get away with shows your autonomy. Even proscriptions against cheating and stealing may be rationalized away. If these modes of pursuing personal advantage do not seem as if they will end up harming you, and you don't really hurt another individual, they may be quite justifiable, and merely demonstrate your independence and resourcefulness:

> ... I wouldn't cheat to a certain point that it would be destructive to me. It would just kind of help in certain ways. You know, for instance, if you've just got a test and you haven't been able to study as much as you wanted.... Let's say I was to swipe the answers from somebody. If I looked

over to the next person and I took two or three answers, I figure it might benefit me in terms of getting over a certain limit, or surpassing the standard I need to surpass, or whatever. And I don't think it'll be hurting the person I took it from really. . . . I figure that in the long run—as long as I know what's going on—as long as I'm not going to continue and this is not going to go overboard or anything—I don't think that's totally bad. If the benefits outweigh the opposite end then I think it's—it's not bad. And like I say it's important to understand what you're doing, and, you know, not to just make it so second nature that you don't even start thinking about it, and then that's how it might get out of hand. . . .

If I get a parking ticket around campus, the last thing I want to do is pay the parking ticket. I feel that, you know, the University should not be doing this to me. And if there's any way I can get something away from the University—for instance, I live off campus, but I've never went out and bought soap. I always come to the school and take it, you know. I figure they've got enough money, this and that. . . .

If somebody at a grocery store gave me back too much change I would not be the person that would say, "Well hold on, you gave me too much change," even though cognitively I know that's the honest thing to do and everything. . . . I think a big part of that is I wouldn't be—it's not like I'm taking it from the cashier or whatever. It's from the store—the big store, so you're kind of—the justification is that they have enough money. They're, you know, a big deal and that sort of thing. For instance, I was in this gift shop in New York with my cousin, and my cousin was going to buy this thing, some basket at this shop. And the woman at the cash register was really busy, and she—I don't know, she must have—she took the gift and she wrapped it—she put it in a bag and gave it to my cousin. And my cousin started to pay, and I said to her, "Well, have you paid yet?"

And she goes, "No, I don't—"

"Well, did she give it back to you?"

"Yeah."

I go, "Well, let's get out of here, then," and we just—we just walked out of the store, you know. . . . But I mean it's not that I go into stores and shoplift all the time, but kind of when—if the opportunity presents itself—it's kind of, if the door is open, you know, I'll use it.

This minimalist sees selective cheating as acceptable because it is in your interest and not really hurting whomever you copy answers from. What's bad—since in that case it could do you harm—is letting the amount of cheating get out of hand. You shouldn't hurt individuals, but getting more for yourself by stealing from institutions or organizations is perfectly reasonable because they are rich. Indeed, it is a good thing to stand up against them. So institutions like universities and stores are fair game to lift things from if the opportunity presents itself. You are showing your independence. Society is just something to outsmart.

If you have access to an organization's funds, as the next speaker does, further liberties may be taken:

I'm treasurer of a club that sets up entertainment after football games, and the conflict always comes in that basically I'm doing everything and running a show and like going out and picking up stuff for a party, say. It's always a question, do I allocate funds to pay for my gas or do I really say, "Well, look, it's my fault for joining," and sort of, you know, absorb it, and at first I did it that way. I was more than willing to give my time and my services and my resources. And slowly I've progressed to the point that I say, "Well, look, if I'm doing that for them, they have to be willing to accept what I'm going to say, and what I say is I need to be repaid in some extent." And it's either gas or whether I stop for lunch, and things along those lines. It's a form of embezzlement I guess, but I always look at it more like—I guess the "opportunity cost" is the best word.

Making use of an organization for personal benefit is what you do if you can. Skimming a little from the top this way, as a kind of self-initiated salary for services rendered, is understood as a perquisite of office. You are entitled to a quid pro quo and can act unilaterally to get it. Embezzlement becomes the exercise of initiative.

What a minimalist can view as being put upon or being a sucker looks very different if a certain kind of social life is understood to be for the common good, and participation in it something that matters in its own right. Such a conception not only can lead to your refraining from cheating or stealing, but to your courting of personal discomfort or worse. This does not automatically make you a zealot who has abdicated all judgment, however. You are bringing your judgment to bear on deciding what constitutes the common good and you are trying to further that, even at personal cost:

> A lot of times you have to be willing to take a risk to make what is a good decision. I'm always getting myself in trouble—not in trouble but just putting myself out on a limb, you know. I don't—I love doing that actually because then it gives me a chance to be righteous. Like I've been involved with politics in my home town from time to time and I had a problem with the last—the latest mayor. I felt that he was doing nothing. It was completely worthless—completely worthless and I was willing to say so. A lot of other people weren't willing to say so because they thought it would make the city look bad if the mayor got impeached or got censured or even if there was a lot of discussion about impeaching him or censuring him.
>
> It's the city manager who runs day-to-day things—the mayor is more to set policy and priorities. But I really felt that he did nothing, and that to allow him to do nothing and get away with it without being reprimanded in any way or form would be a bad thing for the city, simply because it would tell other people you can get away with doing nothing. It would show everyone the city doesn't really care. And so I thought it was very necessary to make some type of statement and so I was the one to put myself out on the limb. I got criticized a lot for it, but I didn't mind because I felt that what I was doing was correct, you know, so it didn't bother me. . . .
>
> A lot of people, I think, see it as a little bit insane, you know, to bother like that. A lot of people don't think about it, which is even worse—they don't think that the decisions they make have an effect on society, that they should be concerned about society in general. Meanwhile I do feel that the decisions I make—not so many that I make now but decisions I'll be

making the rest of my life, or the way I can—the way I *can* make decisions—the way I can influence society is important. You know, I want things to turn out for the best.

Wanting "things to turn out for the best" makes of society more than an arena from which personal advantage is to be extracted by your resourcefulness and initiative. But according to the minimalist outlook, such professed concern for the good of all is merely an ideological cover story. This speaker self-deprecatingly admits to taking pleasure in righteous indignation. Is something like that the real point, so that criticizing the mayor happens to be an idiosyncratic way of pursuing personal gain, on a par with standing up to institutions by beating a parking ticket? Can your real want, as the minimalist assumes, only be to further what is best for you, and not society?

For minimalists, what you want for yourself seems the crucial star to steer by as we navigate among life's events. You are not to let your actions be determined by what society asks of you or what others want. That is not being autonomous. Consider this now in relation to drugs. It may mean for one minimalist rejecting societal pressures against their use. Or it may mean for another minimalist rejecting peer pressure to take them. A speaker talks about never being interested in drugs. The reason for that is finding he has just as good a time at parties as the people who are high:

> Well obviously there's, you know, society's norms for what's right and wrong, and you can either work within those norms if that's the way you want to be or go against them if that's the way you want to be. But it still comes back to—it's got to be right for you. You've got to be doing it for yourself. For instance, I've been approached many times in the past with, "Why don't you try drugs—let's do drugs," you know, which nowadays even though it's illegal, is not—I don't perceive society as saying it's really wrong any more. There's not a real big, "That's a no-no." And I always thought to myself—well, I really was never interested. And so I never tried it. And I have nothing against people who tried it and do it, as long as they're doing it basically because they like it. And it, you know, equates to anything where, if people—you're going to find somebody anywhere who's going to say something you're doing is wrong—something you're doing is right. So it's

just—if you're doing it for yourself because you really feel that way, then I see that as being the most important ethic . . . .

In high school I'd go to the parties and we'd sit around, and, you know, they'd pass a joint around and I'd just pass it on. And every once in a while you'd get the, "Why don't you try, why don't you do this," and I would always say, "I'm not interested," and, you know, "I'm having a fine time as it is." And they would always give me, "Well, OK, that's cool, that's no problem,"—which I thought was very good. I mean I always figured if anybody ever tried to pressure me into something, I'd say, "Forget it," you know, and not be associated with that any more. But it always seemed like as the party went on that I was having just as good a time as anybody else who was high. And so to me it never made a lot of sense. Why go through all the extra hassles? I saw it as being a big hassle, from all standpoints, in that, you know, supply—getting your supplies, having to deal with cops, where are you going to keep it, where are you going to get the money, and things of those lines.

Taking drugs would be a net loss for this speaker. He enjoys himself without them and avoids various hassles like having to worry about the police. If somebody else does find it gratifying enough, then it would make sense to the speaker for that person to take drugs. The point is doing something like that for yourself—because you like the way it makes you feel—and not because of social pressure, such as urging from peers. Again, discerning and acting on what makes you happy, independently of anybody else's telling you what to do, is the highest good. And again, self-focus and autonomy are confounded.

Turn next to another speaker who also rejects drugs. The thinking here contrasts sharply with that of the speaker just considered:

Drugs I feel are wrong, but I'm kind of struggling to—to pinpoint why. I'm not really sure why I think they are. I'm not sure it necessarily goes into the indulgence. . . . It's not even so much an indulgence in selfish things, but it's a negation of—of anything selfless. I'm not so sure that you do it as selfish motives, but you can't operate unselfishly when you don't even have control of self—when you're handing over—when you're alleviating that responsibility. And I just—I guess I feel like that's a responsibility—you are responsible for yourself and you have to assume that in order to function in right and wrong manners. And when you don't assume that, that's almost guaranteeing functioning in wrong ways.

What is against taking drugs for this person is not that the marginal benefit to you is too small relative to your added costs, but that it puts you on the wrong basis in relation to others. As a handing over of control or responsibility for your actions to something alien, you make it harder to act toward others in genuinely useful ways. Autonomy seems to matter just as much to this speaker, but it is autonomy for the purpose of treating others well rather than making yourself happy. Perhaps it is not the case that the only truly independent basis for rejecting drugs is their not being worth it in terms of personal gratification, as with the speaker before last.

For the minimalist, each individual owes others no more than the corollary autonomy to pursue the personal good that one grants oneself. Nothing is to be asked of anyone beyond mutual non-interference:

> I don't have the responsibility to go help people—you know, paint their house, or winterize their homes, although I think that it would be nice if I did. But I don't feel that it's my responsibility. I mean, if they want to winterize their homes, there's ways that they can do it themselves. I do feel it's my responsibility, though, to not infringe on their rights to winterize their homes, or to impede their own self-help, their own efforts to bring up their lives or standard of living or economic status or whatever.
>
> ... My philosophy of life is that, well, OK, these people do need help, but I—let them help themselves, and don't do anything to impede their progress.... There's not a whole lot you can do about a lot of things, so as long as you don't make it worse, I think you're doing a good enough job.

Selfishness may even be rationalized as the best way to help others:

> If you're not going to look out for yourself, who is? You certainly have an obligation to yourself, and the only way you can help others I think is to help yourself as much as possible.

Or the issue may become not so much helping others as defending yourself against them:

> When you're out there, you've gotta keep your guard up. Otherwise, you know, somebody's going to step on *you*. You don't—you don't go out of your way—I don't think I would go out of my way to step on people, or put them back. But you've got to make sure that, you know, you've gotta keep an eye out for yourself and for your own well-being that people don't step—because, when you get right down to it, there're a lot of hungry people or—not in terms of food but just hungry in terms of drive and, you know, ambition—who won't have any qualms about stepping on you.

Seeing others as without claim upon you, looking out for yourself, protecting yourself against assumed predations from others—contrast those with the experience of the following speaker. Here we find an outlook that can lead to absorbing a lot of "unjustified" interference with one's own interests in the service of furthering another's welfare:

> I was sitting in my parked car and all of a sudden, Bang! There was a car that hit behind me. I didn't know what—it hit me—it was a truck, and it was wet and it was raining. And I got out and it was a young man in the car, and he worked for a pest control company. It was a company truck. And he got out and he said—it was like—it was just a rush. He said, "Follow me to so-and-so place," and he hopped in his car and started driving off.

> So I got in the car and started following him. We started going down the street and the next thing I know he was flying down the road at sixty miles an hour. I didn't like what was happening and I thought for sure he was trying to get away from me or something. So I went—had this big car chase and followed him all around.

> Finally he came up and pulled over to the side and I got out. I was very angry with him and I started hollering at him....

He was trying to say, "No, I wasn't running away from you, I wasn't running away from you." And I just—I was quiet and I said, "OK, well what do you have to say?" And he said that he saw his boss coming or something and he was trying to get away from his boss. He wasn't really running away from me. So I didn't know if that was true or not but I figured I had to give him the benefit of the doubt. And then he started telling me how he was high.

I said, "Well, come on back in the car," and we went back to my car. And he's like, you know, he wanted to pay for it himself. He didn't want his boss to find out about it because he would get fired, and he wanted to pay for it himself.... And we're still in the process—I mean, I don't know what's going to happen right now. I don't know whether or not he's going to actually pay for it. He said he was. I told him how much it's going to be and he said, "Well, give me a month." But I question whether or not somebody with his work and pay can get up 800 dollars in a month to pay for a car.

And the whole time I've been like, "Well, what I should have done was just stayed right there," you know, "wait for the cops to come. It would have been taken care of by his company's insurance." And so on and so on. But deep down inside I felt that I couldn't do that to—I couldn't make him lose his job, knowing the way the world is and the economy is, especially when he came to pick me up. His wife had a baby in the car and he seemed to be on the up and up, you know, afterwards....

You know, if it's a middle class person who I knew had money, I probably would have sat there and waited for the cops to come. Or gotten their insurance—they probably would have had insurance. He didn't have insurance. But I think that's what morality is.... I couldn't see making this man lose his job, and—and all the difficulties that would have come onto him because of that, just because I had a dent in the car. It was a big dent, but—but I don't feel that my monetary security in getting the car fixed was more important than that person's—obviously he's going to go through emotional and all kinds of problems with losing his job. And just—his humanity was more important than the car—the material car.

Better to let your guard down and risk loss to yourself. Acting this way whatever the personal outcome is of value to the speaker. Losing money by it would not make it less the thing to do. Is this speaker merely the victim of a tyrannical conscience? This same speaker does in fact talk of discipline in relation to morality—but seems to mean by discipline something very different from tyranny:

> I don't think anything comes—in order to achieve higher levels in anything, you need discipline. If you want to be a good violinist, you have to have good disciplines. If you want to be a good professor, you've got to do a lot of studying, discipline yourself in that. If you want to be a good moral person, you've got to discipline yourself in that. You can't just—one day say, "This is what I want to do as far as morality goes," and do it. You've got to—you discipline yourself, your life style.

Is such talk subterfuge and self-deception if it is understood to mean anything other than willingness to work hard for personal benefit? Must it reflect the impact of some outside agent's imposition unless there is enough in it for you? Can discipline validly mean no more than the self-imposed "torture" of the minimalist who studies hard for tests in order to become a success? Evidently the present speaker sees discipline differently—as rituals or practices undertaken for the sake of something beyond the personal: for music, for knowledge, for morality. Can it only be a distortion to believe you want to serve these in their own right, not as a means to a personal end? Can disciplining yourself in morality only refer to an internalized tyranny rather than a way of cultivating your own wants? Are the minimalists right in identifying autonomy with acting on one's own behalf, deciding for with deciding in favor of one's self, and therefore in justifying limited ethics on the grounds of freedom?

3

Virtue Desired

Many speakers in the preceding pages put autonomy as their first priority and from this deduce the necessity of an ethics aimed—by means short of doing others harm—at benefits to the self. We have called them ethical minimalists. Not to seek personal goals is to allow others to dominate you. Accepting impositions and constraints from outside agencies in any form is the greatest immorality of all. Dignity inheres in resisting the domination of others. More than mutual non-infringement in the pursuit of personal definitions of self-development courts the dangers of subjugation and conformity.

As these people see it, most appeals that are made in the name of ethics simply amount to somebody else or some outside source of putative authority telling them what to do or how to think. Since they find imposition itself to be morally offensive, most of traditional morality has to be rejected by them as cant—at best, well-meaning attempts to "improve" them or "save" them which require the abdication of their own powers, the suspension of their own feelings; at worst, manipulations that seek to legitimate someone else's domination over them by invoking a moral vocabulary.

Minimalists and moral authoritarians agree in understanding the moral enterprise as based upon outside coercion. Where the minimalists reject that coercion, the authoritarians accept it—whether on religious or secular grounds—as desirable and called for. Are those with broader ethics deluded, then, if they believe their morality does not depend upon external sanctions, covertly if not overtly applied? Are the minimalists and the moral authoritarians correct in what they agree on: that moral prescriptions are a result of outside agencies shaping and pressuring the individual? What residues from our intellectual past may have acted to produce such an outlook, and with what warrant?

Moral prescriptions have not always been seen as deriving from external authority—from religious or social forces. Plato and Aristotle held that to be just, self-controlled, and temperate, was what we ourselves really wanted, and was essential to our own well-being and happiness. So did Confucius, in China, and Buddha, in India. For all of these thinkers, we were not to be moral because of what gods or other human beings demanded or imposed. Rather, morality represented something of which we ourselves are the authors, but that we often forget or neglect or are confused about. We need to cultivate our moral tendencies, they asserted, but not in order to satisfy some external authority. We should do so because of what we ourselves most want.

While there is much in the ethical ideas of Plato and Aristotle, and of Buddha and Confucius, with which we disagree— and indeed, much disagreement among these four figures as well— this conception which they held in common seems to us of fundamental importance. A basis for going beyond minimal ethics can be found, we submit, in some of our own desires—desires that are easily lost sight of but that are crucial to our own well-being. Several centuries before the birth of Christ, this was a widely prevalent view of morality. We will now look at the development of this conception in early Greece, and also take a brief glimpse at its representation in the hands of Buddha and Confucius. We will then consider why the conception lost credence, and whether— although not the whole story—it was not on the right track after all.

Greece Before Plato and Aristotle

The views of Plato and Aristotle were actually the culmination of several centuries of earlier Greek thought. We normally tend to take for granted that justice, self-control, and similar virtues are worthy of honor and praise, and that they have always been so regarded. But this was not true of the Greek culture depicted in Homer's *Iliad* and *Odyssey*—several centuries before the eighth century B.C., when they were composed. For the Homeric heroes, "everything pivoted on a single element of honour and virtue: strength, bravery, physical courage, prowess. Conversely, there was no weakness, no unheroic trait, but one, and that was cowardice and the consequent failure to pursue heroic goals." [1]

Let us look at how this changed, to the point of the very different views held by Plato, and then Aristotle. A bit of lexical history will be useful here. The word closest to our "good" in Greek is *agathos*, and that closest to our "virtue" is *arete*. As is still the case for some usages of "good" and "virtue" in English, these terms originally had no particular connection to anything having to do with morality. To say that something or someone was *agathos* (in various linguistic forms) meant, essentially, that they served well a desired end or function. This corresponds to an important non-moral sense of "good" today—as one might speak of a "good knife" or of a "good teacher." *Arete* referred to an excellence or a skill necessary for the performance of a desirable function—as one may say of a knife that it has the "virtue" of sharpness, or of a teacher that he or she has the "virtue" of knowing his or her field. A knife's sharpness lets it cut effectively; a teacher must have knowledge of something in order to be able to teach it.

In Homer's epics, the terms *agathos* and *arete* had a very narrow scope of human application. The kings and chieftains were the only people called *agathos*; indeed, *agathos* could also be used to refer to a king or leader. When *arete* was spoken of with reference to humans, it was almost always the *arete* of the *agathos* that was meant, and this was courage and prowess (in battle and with words). It was these excellences, apart from the prosperity and noble lineage that went with being an *agathos*, that were regarded as essential to performing the function of a king or chieftain.

Then communities grew larger, and a new source of power, money, was introduced. With these new social complexities, the importance of a leader's possessing not only strength and courage, but also such characteristics as justice and honesty, began to reveal itself. Another poet of the eighth century, Hesiod, wrote: "But they who give straight judgments to strangers and to the people of the land, and do not depart from justice—their city flourishes, and the people prosper in it." [2] Hesiod also seems to have realized that it was not only the character of the leader that mattered, but rather that of everyone: "Often even a whole city suffers because of a *kakos* [a poor man] who does wrong." [3]

By the sixth century, another poet proposed that the highest commendation was not to be given to the man with the traditional characteristics of the successful king—noble birth, prosperity, strength, and courage—but to the man who was righteous or just. According to Theognis, "The whole of *arete* is summed up in *dikaiosune* [justice or righteousness]: every man...is *agathos* if he is *dikaios* [just or righteous]." [4]

As the classicist A.W.H. Adkins [5] explains it, Theognis was living at a time of economic and political turmoil when who could claim to be *agathos* and possess *arete* had become a matter of dispute. The real criterion, Theognis saw, was contribution to the well-being and stability of society. And to further this goal, it was justice or righteousness which mattered most of all.

What was seen as most commendable grew to include not only justice but also wisdom and self-control, in addition to courage. One of the characters in Euripides's play *Electra*, written in the fifth century, illustrates the process of broadening that Adkins describes, centering this time on self-control rather than justice. The king Agamemnon has been slain by Aegisthus, who has usurped his throne. Aegisthus has given Agamemnon's daughter Electra to a peasant in marriage, because he feared that if she were to marry a nobleman, this nobleman or a son that Electra might bear from him would avenge his murder of Agamemnon. The peasant shows great consideration for Electra, and has not attempted to consummate the marriage, feeling himself unworthy to do so. Orestes, Electra's brother, has been living in exile and returns to find Electra married to the peasant, whose self-control apparently impresses and amazes him.

Orestes is led to reflect on what really makes a man deserving of praise and honor. He rejects the kinds of standards that traditionally apply to the king or chieftain—physical prowess, noble birth, and wealth: "For this man, who neither has a high position...nor is puffed up by the fame deriving from noble lineage, but is a man of the people, has proved to be *aristos* [most *agathos*]. Will you not come to your senses, you who wander about full of empty opinion, and in future judge men by their mode of life?" [6] A self-controlled mode of life makes for the well-being of social units large or small: "For such men," Orestes goes on to say, "*eu oikein* (administer well) both their cities and their own households." [7]

The Greek value-terms that correspond most closely to our "good" and "virtue" thus started out having nothing to do with morality. What was *agathos* or "good" was what was useful or desirable; what was *arete* or a "virtue" was an excellence necessary for carrying out a desirable function. To say a man was *agathos* or that he possessed *arete* was originally to say that he was a king or leader, or that he possessed what were thought to be the characteristics essential to a successful king or leader—strength and courage. The reference of these terms broadened with the realization that other human qualities were highly desirable as well. They were extended to apply to further traits that are today considered ethical, such as justice and self-control, when it became clear how important these are for the well-being of the group or community.

Plato and Aristotle

The history of *agathos* and *arete* would seem to indicate that when a trait was recognized as beneficial to the group, it became recognized as desirable for the individual as well. But the good of the group is, of course, unfortunately not always identical to the good of the individual. By the fifth century the Sophists and others began to argue—it has a familiar ring—that the individual wouldn't want to be just and self-controlled if social sanctions could be avoided. If you could escape detection, or if you were powerful enough to avoid retribution, then—so the argument went—you were better off ignoring these supposed virtues, and getting what you could for yourself.

Callicles, as portrayed by Plato, expressed this position particularly clearly. He sounds much like Nietzsche did twenty-three centuries later: the powerless "praise temperance and justice by reason of their own unmanliness." If a man is in a position to seize power, for him to impose on himself "a master in the shape of the law, the talk and the rebuke of the multitude," would be bound to lead him to wretchedness. "Luxury and licentiousness and liberty, if they have the support of force, are virtue and happiness, and the rest of these embellishments—the unnatural covenants of mankind—are all mere stuff and nonsense." [8]

Much of Plato's writing on ethics was aimed at showing that such a view was in error. His thrust in this regard can be seen as a kind of defense and culmination of the development of earlier Greek thinking about *arete*. What was *arete* had always been something everyone would desire; and justice, temperance, and self-control—as well as wisdom—had all come to be viewed as kinds of *arete* in addition to courage. Callicles and others were now arguing that these ethical qualities did not really represent *arete* after all.

Socrates—whom a great deal of Plato's work centered on expounding—sought to show that being just, temperate, and self-controlled was good not only for the group but for the individual. Socrates tried to demonstrate that treating others in a just manner is more beneficial personally than acting unjustly, even if no one knows of the injustice and there is no punishment for it. Justice—and also temperance and other virtues—were, he argued, essential to a person's health and well-being: "It is by the possession of justice and temperance that the happy are happy and by that of vice the wretched are wretched." [9]

Furthermore, according to Socrates, people always aim to pursue the good. "No one," he said, "willingly goes after evil or what he thinks to be evil; it is not in human nature, apparently, to do so—to wish to go after what one thinks to be evil in preference to the good; and when compelled to choose one of two evils, nobody will choose the greater when he may the lesser." [10] It is easy to make mistakes in your conception of what is good and evil, but to pursue the former and avoid the latter is always what you really want. Problems stem from error—confusion or insufficient knowledge.

In Socrates' and Plato's thinking about ethics, the traditional Greek gods were not significant. Most of these gods in fact cared little about mere human beings, except for the sacrifices, offerings, and honors which they felt mortals owed them. Apollo says to Poseidon in Homer's *Iliad*, "I should not be sensible if I fought with you on account of wretched mortals, who like leaves now flourish, as they eat the fruit of the field, and now fade away lifeless." [11] Plato did adopt some concepts that could be called religious or perhaps supernatural or mystical. He envisioned a transcendent realm of eternal "Ideas" or "Forms" beyond the world of ever-changing sensory experience, and conceived of human beings as possessing immortal souls that strive towards the Form of goodness. But he seems to have believed, with Socrates, that the good was what we ourselves always really desired, quite apart from such notions as these.

With Aristotle there is even less tendency to base ethics in religion. Aristotle defined the good directly in terms of our desires. His *Nicomachean Ethics* begins with the question: what is the good for human beings? The answer given is *eudaimonia*—usually translated as "happiness" or "well-being," perhaps more accurately as "the best possible life," where "best" does not mean "morally best" but rather "what we all most want." [12] Most of the rest of the book then spells out what Aristotle regards as the various virtues—among which justice, temperance, and self-control are prominent—all of which he sees as conducive to, and necessary for, the kind of life we all most want, or *eudaimonia*.

Aristotle disagreed with some of what Socrates had said. He thought that the view that no one ever chooses what they know to be evil rather than good (which Plato himself gave up in his later writing) "plainly contradicts the observed facts." [13] People sometimes do opt for known evils—even though it is against their real interests to do so. What you "know" in an abstract sense is not always appropriately in the forefront of your mind, determining your behavior. Knowledge is not enough if you don't take it into account before acting, and you can be overcome by the passions of the moment. But for Aristotle no less than for Socrates and Plato, evil was never in line with what you really wanted, while the good always was.

They were all convinced that we would invariably choose what is just or otherwise good, if we were acting with full knowledge and rationality. To be just, temperate, in control of oneself—such forms of conduct were desirable not only for the group but also for each individual. Our own preference will always be to act ethically, except when we are misled by lack of understanding or other limitations.

That Plato and Aristotle saw ethics as based on human desires did not mean, however—as it tends to mean for modern humanists—that they simply expected human beings to behave ethically, so long as external forces did not constrain them or lead them astray. Plato and Aristotle both thought of ethical conduct as something that very much had to be worked on or cultivated. They did not at all believe that what came spontaneously from within was always good, and that the sources of evil all came from the outside.

Plato was especially concerned with the way in which ignorance and confusion stand in the way of our ethical conduct. The dialogues aimed at dispelling these and improving the quality of people's thinking about matters related to morality. Again and again, Socrates asks questions like, "What is justice?" "What is temperance?" And he then proceeds to make his companions realize that they do not themselves really believe what they thought they did about such matters. He does not know the true answers either, he says; he cannot simply supply them. But Socrates—as Plato describes him—certainly seemed convinced that by engaging in such a dialectic process, thinking and searching, we would come closer to valid ideas—and that this was crucial to conducting ourselves well in the world.

Aristotle, in turn, did not think that the main cause of moral failure was confusion and ignorance. We are often misled by pleasure and by passion, in spite of what we in some sense "know." What was required, according to Aristotle, was the development of moral character. Moral qualities "are in a certain sense natural attributes" already within us. [14] But we need to form appropriate habits, and this takes disciplined practice. By accustoming ourselves to acting justly, temperately, and bravely, we develop a just, temperate, and brave character. "It makes no small difference," said Aristotle, "whether we form habits of one kind or another from our very youth; it makes a very great difference, or rather *all* the difference." [15]

Plato and Aristotle were thus both in strong disagreement with the view of most modern humanists: that we would always spontaneously behave ethically provided only that we have the freedom to do so. They saw our actions as often misguided—whether by ignorance and confusion, or by pleasure and passion. Ethical conduct is something we need to work at. It is not just there, but has to be cultivated. It requires learning or practice on our part, the aim of which is to gain wisdom or to develop character. Yet it is congruent with our real wants.

There is much that Plato and Aristotle said about ethics with which today it seems impossible to agree. Certainly some of the *content* of what they viewed as ethically good seems unacceptable. Among other problems, they accepted slavery, they had a very restricted definition of who constituted "citizens," and these philosophers serenely maintained that clearly what was most conducive to *eudaimonia* was doing philosophy.

More critical for our central concerns, Plato and Aristotle both believed in a closer relationship between ethical conduct and what the individual most wants than seems defensible. Plato even went so far as to argue that virtue was all that really mattered for one's happiness. Aristotle thought this went too far: a virtuous man could suffer great misfortunes and no one would call him happy "unless he were maintaining a thesis at all costs." [16] But neither Plato nor Aristotle seems to have confronted the possibility that what is ethically best may not always coincide with what, even "really," the individual most wants.

Unless one gives up the idea that ethics has to do with consideration for others—its most crucial core as we see it—faith in such coinciding seems by now over-optimistic to say the least. Could one hope to attribute all the evil we human beings have perpetrated in the world to our failure to act on what we really want? But on the other hand, does it not seem correct to say that we do want to be ethical beings? While Plato and Aristotle may have erred by neglecting possible conflicts with other desires that we also possess, they do not seem to us to be wrong in their view that the individual really has wants in such directions as justice and self-control. If we ourselves want things of these kinds—although they are not *all* we want, and some of our desires can be contradictory—this would seem important to recognize.

You may find objectionable the notion that an individual may not always know his or her own real desires. To allow that people may be mistaken in what they think they want is to open the door to the danger of someone else's telling them what that really is. And yet, it seems clear that we *can* make mistakes here. Who has not sometimes realized, too late, that he or she would have been better off without something they thought they desperately wanted—a particular job change, a particular purchase? The problem is perhaps not in the idea that we sometimes lack knowledge of our real desires. This may be true enough. The problem rather may lie in the idea of handing over to anyone else the responsibility for doing something about it. Instead, we can carefully and concretely envision the implications of possible actions.

Actually, it is a very common notion in contemporary Western society that you may be misled about your own desires—only usually your real motives are taken to be worse, not better, than the ones you think you have. Freud has accustomed us to the view that human beings think of themselves as better than they really are. But may not the opposite occur as well? Especially under the influence of prevailing social science ideologies, with their emphasis on the debunking of apparent virtue, may we not sometimes fail to recognize in ourselves wishes to be just, wishes for the common good and the good of others, that we in fact possess?

We believe—and much of the rest of this book will be concerned with showing—that human beings do have desires of this kind. That we have them seems an important fact about us. They serve as the basis, in our view, for going beyond a minimal ethic, quite apart from any matters of religion.

Indeed, it is hard to see how, in the absence of religion, more than a minimal ethic makes any sense, unless we do have desires of this kind. Why *should* we then behave justly or honestly where injustice or dishonesty on our part would escape detection, or generously where we do not expect any rewards? "To soothe your conscience," is not a satisfactory answer. If my conscience is only something that has been arbitrarily implanted in me by my culture, then Callicles, and more recently Nietzsche, would seem to be quite right that to obey it is to accept an imposition on myself, to give in to weakness. It is only if I really want the good that my conscience represents, that I can wish—as an act of strength, not weakness, of autonomy, not conformity—to obey it. It is not surprising that ethics are limited when people do not recognize themselves as having any fundamental desires besides those of their own self-interest.

Buddha and Confucius

In the same time period as the developments in Greece that we have been considering, two men in the far removed lands of India and China were also claiming close relationships between ethics and what human beings really want: Buddha and Confucius. Consider Buddha first.

Buddha saw the cause of our pain and sufferings as our egoistic cravings. We could overcome our sufferings, he maintained, by freeing ourselves of these cravings. He proposed a path to the cessation of suffering in which, along with meditation and the attainment of a broader perspective, ethical conduct plays a central role. An important part of the path was to understand good and evil and live accordingly.

What was regarded as good and evil has striking similarities to what is so regarded in the Judeo-Christian tradition. One account in the early Buddhist scriptures of what is evil—not unlike the familiar Ten Commandments—lists killing, stealing, unlawful sexual intercourse, lying, slandering, using harsh language, vain talk, covetousness, cruelty, and "wrong views." [17] These scriptures contain many sayings like "Let a man overcome hatred by kindness, evil by goodness, greed by generosity, and lies by telling the truth." [18] Or again, "Let a man practice a boundless goodwill for all the world." [19]

Buddha was quite explicit that your evil causes you misery, and your good, happiness. According to another saying, "If a man speak or act with an evil thought, suffering follows him as a wheel follows the hoof of the beast that draws the cart. . . . If a man speak or act with a good thought, happiness follows him like a shadow that never leaves him." [20]

Rather like Socrates, Buddha thought you needed to overcome your misunderstandings about the world and about yourself. The main way he thought you could do this was by meditation. You are to become aware of the true nature of things, including their transitoriness, and when you do so, you will realize that the egoistic satisfactions you have been seeking are not important and not what you really want.

While for Plato and Aristotle morality is clearly related to what we desire, there is a problem in saying anything quite like this for Buddha. Desires seem to be something we are to give up—although perhaps Buddha really only intended us to give up egoistic desires. But in any case, it is, if anything, even more clear for Buddha than for Plato and Aristotle, that we are often in error as to what we really want, and that this is especially true when we act without good will, in ways that harm others.

But we mean to be talking about morality that is independent of religion here, and was not Buddha preaching religion? In the usual senses of the term, he in fact was not. Buddha opposed reliance on authority, tradition, and ritual, said nothing about a god, and in general emphasized direct experience and eschewed speculation. If it is religion to hold that the way we tend to see the world is largely illusory, that we should strive to see it aright, and that we are misguided as to what we think we want, then certainly Buddha's outlook would be called a religious one. Note, however, that such an outlook is not altogether different from views more often heard today in the name of science. In particular, the idea that we are often seriously in error as to our real desires is, as already mentioned, widely current in psychology—although the errors psychologists claim we make lie in a very different direction.

Further and more critically, Buddha's "religion," if that is what we should call it, has a very different relationship to ethics than what we are used to. You are not being asked to follow commandments of God or any other authority. Indeed, the Buddhist scriptures represent Buddha as warning his followers not to be misled by report or tradition or even by their teacher. [21] You are being urged towards better understanding, and it is expected that you will then yourself realize that your selfish desires are not significant and not what you really want. This is also very different from providing you with a new motive for being ethical, such as the existence of a heaven and hell: you are to become aware of—and act upon—the motives you possess already.

Actually, Buddha apparently did propose a further additional incentive as well. He seems to have accepted the ancient doctrine of reincarnation or continual rebirth, and held that you could be released from this otherwise endless cycle and its suffering by following the path he recommended. But it seems clear that the practices he urged were expected to lead to a decrease of suffering not only in some hypothetical future, but *now*, in *this* life. It was in fact by your own experiences of that decrease in suffering, here and now, that you were to know for yourself what was good. [22]

A beautiful example of the way in which giving up egoistic cravings can be directly experienced as leading to reduction of suffering is provided, quite without any thought of its relation to Buddhist doctrine, by the psychologist Fritz Heider. Heider has become renowned for a book on interpersonal relations, which gave rise to a whole new line of work in social psychology. In his autobiography he describes how, when he was first elaborating his ideas on interpersonal relations, he became frustrated by the lack of time he had available to work on them. He developed attacks of anxiety, which seemed only to grow worse as he struggled against them. Then he told himself it was not so crucial whether these ideas of his came to fruition or not: "I am not so important. Other people are much more important, and there are many more of them!" [23] And the attacks of anxiety ceased. Happily (although Buddhist practices probably cannot be given the credit here) he soon thereafter received a fellowship and a new job offer that enabled him to devote more time to his ideas.

At nearly the same time as Buddha, Confucius—in China—was also urging the importance of moral practices, and on grounds that had nothing to do with religion. One of Confucius's sayings is, "We don't know yet how to serve men, how can we know about serving the spirits?" [24] It was emphatically on human nature rather than on the gods that morality was to be based.

A follower of Confucius named Mencius—generally regarded as representing the "orthodox" Confucian tradition—put very clearly the role of our nature and also the role of cultivation of that nature: "Charity, righteousness, propriety, and moral consciousness are not something that is drilled into us; we have got them originally with us, only we often forget about them (or neglect or ignore them). Therefore it is said, 'Seek and you will find it, neglect and you will lose it.'" [25]

Confucius—when he could get a hearing from them—was most of all concerned with counselling rulers and officials to set a good moral example, and to seek peace and the common good. (He would have his work cut out for him today.) He put less stress on the relationship between an individual's ethical conduct and his or her happiness or suffering, but he too believed in such a relationship—in much the same way as Plato. Another of Confucius's sayings is, "He who is really good is never unhappy." [26]

As with Plato and Aristotle, there are many aspects of what Buddha and Confucius said about ethics with which one could take issue. For example, Confucius thought of human relationships very much in hierarchical terms, not at all as involving equality; Buddha may have encouraged more withdrawal from the creatures and problems of our earth than seems desirable. More critical here, neither Buddha nor Confucius, any more than Plato and Aristotle, seems to have seriously considered that what is ethically best and what is best for the individual may not always coincide.

But again, it seems to us a correct and important insight of Buddha and Confucius that ethics can be founded on what human beings really want. We will present more arguments for this later. For the moment, what we hope to have established is that Plato, Aristotle, Buddha, and Confucius all held this view. Morality—in contrast to the way it is understood in so much of social science—was not seen by them as something that has to be imposed on us from the outside.

At the same time—in contrast to the outlook typical of modern humanism—morality was not seen by them as something that will simply develop spontaneously without any need for specific effort on its behalf. The good was something you really wanted—but that was not enough to assure its prevailing. You did not just automatically always think of it, know what it was, and pursue it. Plato, Aristotle, Buddha, and Confucius all viewed ethical conduct as something you had to work at, although in different ways.

To Confucius, what you most needed would seem to be a kind of consciousness-raising. The basis for ethics is already there within us, but we have to look for it—it is easily forgotten or neglected. Plato and Buddha, in turn, were particularly concerned with overcoming the misunderstandings that they saw as keeping us from pursuing the good: Plato, largely by means of thought and dialogue, Buddha, by means of meditation. And Aristotle maintained that we especially needed to form habits of acting virtuously—practice was required. They all believed, in the words of a Zen Buddhist many centuries later, that "virtues are the fruit of self-discipline and do not drop from heaven of themselves as does rain or snow." [27] Recall the student who, in chapter 2, says, "If you want to be a good moral person, you've got to discipline yourself in that. You can't just—one day say, 'This is what I want to do as far as morality goes,' and do it."

Today, in the modern West, morality is not often seen as something that we ourselves really want and that we develop through efforts at discipline and cultivation. It tends to be regarded either as originating outside us—something toward which we have to be bent—or as something that will, under conditions of freedom, just come about naturally and spontaneously. The conception of morality common to Plato, Aristotle, Buddha, and Confucius came to be rejected. Were there good reasons for this?

We think not. Rather, as will be considered next, what seems to have happened is that religious developments led to placing the source of morality outside of ourselves. With the elaboration of Christian doctrines, it came to be widely believed that little or no good was to be found originally in human nature. What was good about us had to be of divine authorship. When faith in religion then declined, this belief in the poverty of our natures, paradoxically enough, often remained. Many students of human conduct—among them Freudian psychoanalysts, social learning theorists, and behavior modifiers—continued to regard human nature as quite inadequate to provide a foundation for morality. God had to be replaced by social constraint. Others—among them the neo-Freudians, humanistic psychologists like Abraham Maslow and Carl Rogers, and other humanists—did return to the view that we had the bases of morality within ourselves. But they were so concerned with the danger of any kinds of constraints on our natures, that they quite lost sight of the possibility that what was good in them might require work and efforts at cultivation.

4

The Mystification of Goodness

Current Western understandings of ethics have little in common with those of Plato and Aristotle. They thought of the good as something everybody wants, though we often fail to act in terms of it because of ignorance or confusion or insufficient self-discipline. Our own desires will lead us to be just, to be honest, to consider the well-being of others, when limitations in understanding or discipline do not impede our exercise of these inclinations. Such an outlook clearly encourages having morality on our minds—the putting of much effort into discerning and acting upon moral considerations in a wide range of what we do, quite apart from whether or not there are external sanctions.

Giving moral considerations this kind of centrality often is opposed these days on principle. As we argued in chapter 1, a minimalist ethic arose as an effect of liberalism's attention to the autonomy of the individual. What seemed unsupportable except at the price of that autonomy was anything beyond mutual toleration for people's going by their feelings and pursuing any ends as equally valid, as long as they did not hurt others. Believing spontaneity of feelings or personal fulfillment to be itself morally good but for deformations imposed on us by environmental forces, or at least to be in the direction of mental health, much in current psychology encourages, in the name of autonomy, that ethical prescriptions be minimized. To call someone "judgmental" is understood to be a form of criticism—an accusation of intolerance.

Contemporary philosophy, despairing of finding a foundation for justifying ethics, has for the most part fitted right into this picture, viewing morality as essentially a matter of individual attitude or unfounded choice. For minimalists, morality is in the last analysis whatever way we happen to feel, unamenable to further defense. And many speakers who expressed this view to us seemed to invoke freedom or autonomy as their grounding.

Those writers who decry the selfishness that seems thereby legitimated often end up, implicitly or explicitly, ready to sacrifice autonomy as a necessary price to pay for the rediscovery of community. They sense as romantic illusion the claim that self-expression and spontaneity will work out for the good of all. Authoritarian grounds for morality are offered—the sanctions of divine or temporal presences. Broader ethics are understood as calling for the undercutting of our wants or desires. We must submit our will to that of God, and out of faith in religious dicta seek the welfare of others. Or we must submit to secular authorities—our parents and other "agents of socialization"—who design contingencies that will impinge on us to our detriment if we do not further altruistic and communal ends.

These contingencies of socialization may in turn become self-administering, in the form of "conscience." Now we approve or disapprove of ourselves where before it took others. But conscience, understood as our taking over the work of agents of socialization on their behalf, is then no more than our having ceded autonomy inside our heads as well as outside. We have internalized the sanctions of those with power over us—broader ethics once again then depending on yielding to authority, and qualms of conscience becoming the sentiment of cowardice. Yet many with broad ethics who spoke with us hardly seemed the slaves of internalized sanctions.

What went wrong? Why is it that now more than a minimal ethic is widely understood to require support from religion or from social sanctions, though for Plato, Aristotle, Buddha, and Confucius it did not? What led to the decline of their views? How is it that the good, which they saw as something that everybody really seeks but that cannot be achieved without working on ourselves to act accordingly, came to be seen either as something that requires God or the sanctions of society, or else as something to be achieved through spontaneity, for which no special efforts need to be made? The answer, we submit, is to be found in the history of Judeo-Christian thinking. It lies in the way Western religion affected our view of morality and of ourselves.

The Good as God's Commands

Contrary to what is frequently taken for granted, religion in most early cultures did not seem to start out with morality-enhancing characteristics, but rather to take these on subsequently.[1] To begin with, the gods were to be propitiated as a way of avoiding otherwise uncontrollable misfortunes. Our behavior to one another—as among the ancient Greeks—was usually not of great concern to the gods, who were often capricious, and sometimes positively malevolent. But Egyptian tombs built about four and a half thousand years ago already referred to the meting out of divine judgment on moral grounds. On the tomb of Harkuf of Elephantine are inscribed the words: "I gave bread to the hungry, clothing to the naked, I ferried him who had no boat.... I was one saying good things and repeating what was loved. Never did I say aught evil to a powerful one against anybody." And the reason? "I desired that it might be well with me in the Great God's presence."[2]

The Egyptians went on to develop a detailed conception of judgment after death, portrayed graphically in the Book of the Dead. The heart of the deceased is weighed in a balance to determine what future fate is deserved. Declaring innocence, the petitioner proclaims "I have committed no sin against people.... I allowed no one to hunger. I caused no one to weep. I did not murder. I did not command to murder. I caused no man misery."[3] Eligibility for reward in an afterlife depended on sustaining such a case.

Also, almost two thousand years before Christ, the sun-god Shamash was portrayed as calling upon the Babylonian king Hammurabi to establish the code of laws that bears his name.[4] Most of the Babylonian gods were thought of as self-centered and uncaring about how human beings treated each other, but Shamash was different. There is a hymn which begins, "Oh Shamash, out of thy net no evil-doer escapes, Out of thy snare no sinner flees."[5] The good was coming to be viewed as something that particular gods expected of us.

The identification of ethics with divine commands became thorough among the ancient Jews. They saw Yahweh as the one true God, whose greatest concerns were justice and righteousness, and who stood ready to unleash doom upon anyone who transgressed his moral law. This law—understood to have been given to Moses when he led the Jews out of Egypt (about 1200 B.C.)—places much emphasis on consideration for others, especially for the poor and the needy. The Ten Commandments are a part of it, as are such statements as, "If there is among you a poor man...you shall open your hand to him, and lend him sufficient for his need, whatever it may be."[6]

During the ancient period, many groups in and around the Mediterranean region had national gods who looked out for their particular people, in return for which these gods demanded rituals and offerings. Yahweh may have begun as such a national god, but with the growth of moral consciousness that took place among the Jews as among the Greeks and many other peoples during the middle part of the last millenium B.C. (in the Mediterranean basin and elsewhere), he became more and more clearly the one and only God, who thundered condemnation and retribution upon anyone who oppressed the poor or took advantage of the weak.

The moral concern and the outrage at injustice felt by Jewish prophets and other leaders were attributed by them to Yahweh—to the God who had saved them from the Egyptians and brought them to the land of Canaan. The prophet Amos (about 750 B.C.) presents God as infuriated with the powerful of Israel, "because they sell the righteous for silver, and the needy for a pair of shoes—they that trample the head of the poor into the dust of the earth, and turn aside the way of the afflicted."[7] God says, according to Amos, "I hate, I despise your feasts, and I take no delight in your solemn assemblies. Even though you offer me your burnt offerings and cereal offerings, I will not accept them, and the peace offerings of your fatted beasts I will not look upon. Take away from me the noise of your songs; to the melody of your harps I will not listen. But let justice roll down like waters, and righteousness like an everflowing stream."[8]

By the 500s B.C., the second Isaiah clearly presents the morally passionate God as the single mighty Lord of all creation: "I am the Lord, and there is no other. I form light and create darkness, I make weal and create woe, I am the Lord, who do all these things. Shower, O heavens, from above, and let the skies rain down righteousness."[9]

The law of God was not generally understood to be an imposed burden, onerous to carry out. It was often spoken of as a welcome gift you were granted, something you loved and delighted in. It was celebrated with lyrical appreciation as that which enabled you to reach the heights of your own powers. Perhaps an avid chess player might feel a little the same way about the rules of the game of chess, or a musical composer about the laws of harmony. A Psalm expresses the feeling well: "The law of the Lord is perfect, reviving the soul; the testimony of the Lord is sure, making wise the simple; the precepts of the Lord are right, rejoicing the heart; the commandment of the Lord is pure, enlightening the eyes . . . the ordinances of the Lord are true, and righteous altogether. More to be desired are they than gold, even much fine gold; sweeter also than honey and drippings of the honeycomb." [10]

God's law was not something separate and distinct from what made for human well-being. Our welfare was what God wanted and what the law was for. But ethics was becoming divinized. Among the people who became the Jews, religion came to play an increasing role in the guidance of human conduct.

The development of the Jewish wisdom literature itself illustrates this, though it occurred mostly after much of ethics had already become a matter of religion. The early proverbs encourage learning how one should live by the use of one's eyes and ears and reason. [11] Job, by the sixth or fifth century, questions whether this is possible: "But where shall wisdom be found? And where is the place of understanding? Man does not know the way to it, and it is not found in the land of the living." [12] By about two centuries before Christ, Sirach, in Ecclesiasticus, [13] has identified wisdom with God's law. And in The Wisdom of Solomon, a little later, it is even said that "the reasoning of mortals is worthless" [14]—with wisdom, instead of being something you search for, being something you pray for. [15]

The Jews did not, of course, stop trying to reason about how to conduct oneself in life. But it was coming to be God and not our desires that defined the good.

The Severing of Virtue from Human Desire

Starting several centuries before the birth of Christ, the entire Mediterranean region experienced a long period of conquests, the breakdown of communities, and a great deal of strife. With upheaval all around, the testimony of one's eyes and ears and reason did not seem auspicious as a means for human betterment. There was a quite general decline of faith in human wisdom and judgment.

Doubts grew about the possibilities that this life afforded. What came to matter most was no longer anything having to do with the ordinary natural world of our everyday lives, as understood through our senses and faculties. It became common to focus on a higher, supernatural world of the spirit—a divine world—beyond the natural one. Increasing numbers came to think about the attainment of happiness not now, but beyond the grave. "Mystery religions" flourished, with secret initiation ceremonies that involved a kind of spiritual rebirth in a mystical union with a deity who had died and then risen again. People felt they could not rely on themselves but had to turn elsewhere. Guides for this quest abounded. There was "a profusion of holy men, quacks, miracle workers, priests, astrologers, magicians, eastern savants, suffering saints, theatrical Cynics, Stoic vegetarians, divinized Emperors, and a rich clutch of charms, tables, [magic] recipes, and prayers." [16]

The views of Jews and Greeks intermingled with one another and with those of other groups as well. Ironically enough, some of the focus on the supernatural took fuel from certain aspects of Plato's thinking. As we mentioned in chapter 3, Plato believed that beyond the objects of the perceptible world, with their continual variation and changes, there is a higher, unchanging, realm of "Ideas" or "Forms," like those of justice and goodness. Our usual experience is like that of prisoners in a cave, fettered in such a way that they are unable to look out, but can see only shadows thrown on the rear wall within. [17] These shadows on the cave's wall, cast by objects—invisible to the prisoners—moved about behind their backs and illuminated by a fire still further behind them, are what they take as reality. Our everyday perceptions are like such shadows would be for the prisoners, and the Idea of goodness is from their perspective like the sun. It belongs to a realm altogether removed from that which we normally inhabit—a source of light of which we have only the remotest indications.

The good, the moral, came increasingly to be understood as belonging essentially not to our human, natural world but to the higher realms. The Jews had already for a long time been thinking of moral rules as commands of God. These commands had been thought to further what was good for us, but now to many people such a human referent came to seem of less and less significance.

Moreover, we ourselves were coming to be seen as fundamentally lacking in goodness. It was already asked in the Book of Job, "What is man, that he can be clean? Or he that is born of a woman, that he can be righteous?" [18] With Christianity, this view of our own evil took hold more strongly. The Apostle Paul said, in the New Testament, "I know that nothing good dwells within me." [19] It became a fundamental tenet that we were all of us sinners, and incapable without divine help of overcoming sin. The reason Christ had come was to redeem us from our sinfulness, and the conception of this sinfulness was built into the whole system of rituals and sacraments of the Church.

Not only were we constantly sinning, but sinning could itself be gratifying, quite apart from whatever it accomplished—as Augustine illustrated in the description of his theft of some pears in his youth: "For, having plucked them, I threw them away, my sole gratification in them being my own sin, which I was pleased to enjoy. For if any of those pears entered my mouth, the sweetener of it was my sin in eating it." [20] He was horrified at himself, "that I should be gratuitously wanton, having no inducement to evil but the evil itself. It was foul, and I loved it... I loved my own error—not that for which I erred, but the error itself." [21]

The Christian concept of sin is far removed from the thinking of Plato and Aristotle. Plato and Aristotle did not believe that you were always moral. But when you were not, this was because you did not understand, or because you were overcome by some lapse of passion, or were following bad habits. It made no sense to choose purposely anything other than the good: the good was what you really wanted. But now the good had become what God asked of you instead. It had been made into something outside of and apart from you. Now you could purposely choose evil—and often did.

Just how corrupt we actually are was not a matter on which all Christians held the same opinion. For many centuries, belief in our sinfulness, while never absent, was typically attenuated by the consideration that God had, after all, created us. With the rise of Protestantism in the sixteenth century, conviction of the total evil of our nature became much more widespread. It was a crucial part of Luther's doctrine that we must recognize our utter depravity and see that all good came only from God. Then, and only then, could we be saved.

The connection between virtue and what we naturally want had been progressively weakened. Ethics had become divinized, the divine had become more distinct from the earthly, and human nature had become increasingly depraved. The good could no longer be defined in terms of natural human desires.

The Philosophers

Not everyone was content to leave ethics dependent on religion. By the period of the Enlightenment quite a number of thinkers began looking seriously for a basis for ethics apart from God. Though most people were still strongly religious, skepticism had arisen about many religious doctrines, among them that of original sin. No rational means could be seen for resolving the differences which had begun to proliferate among the various Christian sects. On the other hand, Newton and other scientists had demonstrated the power of human understanding. General optimism about the species was returning, and there was a new belief in progress. Many philosophers now thought that it should be possible to establish morality on a foundation other than religion, and proceeded to try to do so.

Their efforts, it is generally agreed, did not succeed, nor have such efforts succeeded since. [22] Except for those who can respond in terms of religion, most people today do not really seem to have a compelling answer to the question, "Why should I go beyond a minimal ethic?" As we have seen, those who emphasize the importance of individual autonomy often say in effect that there is no answer. It is a matter of arbitrary choice: different people seek different ends and, infringements on others excepted, you cannot make value judgments about what they seek. Many for whom religion itself is unacceptable because of its claims on their autonomy feel that this is the only outlook available to them. They may or may not regret its selfish implications, but their commitment to preserving autonomy gives them, in their view, no recourse.

Others urge that the answer is externally imposed sanctions for morality. Selfishness must be countered by secular if not religious sources of authority. People must be more strongly "socialized"—broader ethics must be supported by society's power over the individual, and this power must become internalized in the form of society's representative within the individual, our consciences. Self-appraisals must become more strongly dependent on society's appraisals—in effect, the ultimate breach of our autonomy, the plunder of our minds through manipulation of the grounds for guilt and self-regard. The price of ethics is ceding autonomy, and it must be paid. But that price tag can make ethics seem an ill-affordable luxury.

Why was a basis not found in the autonomous individual for more than a minimal ethic? Why did it not seem possible to base ethics once again, as the Greeks had done earlier in the history of our civilization, on our own natures?

A large part of the problem, we will argue, is that those who now sought a basis for ethics apart from God—even when they rejected the idea of our sinfulness, or rejected religion altogether—still retained much of the conception of morality that they had inherited from the Christian tradition. What was good had been, in Christianity, the carrying out of God's desires, as opposed to our own. It could not now readily become again what we ourselves wanted.

At first, the justification of ethics without recourse to God did not seem so difficult—at least to some, flushed with the optimism of the Enlightenment. Was not morality eminently reasonable? Could it not be based on our rationality? Samuel Clarke, for example, maintained that "he that refuses to deal with all men equitably, is guilty of the very same unreasonableness and contradiction in one Case, as he that in another Case should affirm one Number or Quantity to be equal to another, and yet That other at the same time not to be equal to the first." [23] Spinoza believed that a complete ethics could be logically deduced from definitions and self-evident axioms, and went on to write such an ethics, in the form of a system of geometry. [24]

David Hume, however, soon pointed out a serious problem: rationality by itself does not tell you what to do in the world—it does not give you ends to strive for. "The ultimate ends of human action," he said, "can never, in any case, be accounted for by *reason*." [25] Ask someone why he exercises, Hume continues, and he will answer that he exercises because he wants to keep his health. Ask why he desires health, and he may say, because sickness is painful and he hates pain. To the question why he hates pain, he cannot give a further answer. Or suppose he says he desires health because it is necessary for pursuing his work. If you ask why that is important, he may say, because he wants to obtain money, and to your next "Why?" he may answer that money is the means to pleasure. "Beyond this it is an absurdity to ask for a reason. It is impossible there can be a progress *in infinitum*; and that one thing can always be a reason why another is desired. Something must be desirable on its own account." [26]

Hume argued that reason is powerless to justify any kind of behavior unless ultimately "something desirable on its own account" will be achieved. Thus, if you care about nothing beyond your own narrow interests, reason would be unable to convince you not to take advantage of others if you could avoid reprisals, or not to lie to them if you could get away with it—let alone to be kind or generous, or to choose a life plan that explicitly tries to further the good of others. Reason can play a role in ethical behavior only to the extent that you already have relevant desires which reason can help you to fulfill or understand more adequately.

No one has ever succeeded in getting around this problem, though many efforts have been made and are still being made. Kant believed that insofar as we were rational, we would behave according to his "categorical imperative": "Act only on that maxim whereby thou canst at the same time will that it should become a universal law." [27] A good case can indeed be made that you cannot consistently regard a mode of behavior as moral for yourself if you would not regard it as moral for everyone else under the same circumstances. But this has no implications for how I should act unless I want to be moral.

Suppose, for example, I am in some kind of trouble from which I can extricate myself by making a promise I do not intend to keep. If everyone were to make deceitful promises under such circumstances, Kant says, then promises would soon become meaningless. [28] But why—apart from any wish on my part to be fair or ethical—should this affect my action? Even assuming that, out of enlightened self-interest, I want promises to remain meaningful and promise-making to continue, I could still quite rationally make a false one myself. I would merely be motivated to cover up my deception. There is nothing irrational in doing something you would not be willing for others to do, unless being fair and ethical matter to you in the first place.

Some have thought that the notion of a social contract can provide a rational grounding for morality, or at least for justice. What would we all agree to, if there were no society yet and we as potential members were trying to establish what its principles should be? What sort of social order would we all find acceptable, if the slate were wiped clean and we were ignorant of the personal positions we were to occupy? The basic idea is that the principles we would arrive at under some circumstances of this kind would be just ones. But even assuming that we could determine such principles and that they would be just, rationality will again not require my following them unless I have a wish to be just. Thus John Rawls, who has recently elaborated a highly influential version of social contract theory, [29] does not see the principles he propounds as ones we must necessarily obey if we are to be rational, but rather as ones that articulate and integrate our convictions about what justice entails. [30]

Most contemporary philosophers have given up the enterprise of justifying morality on the grounds of rationality, though a few are still attempting to do so. Alan Gewirth, [31] who has probably made the clearest and most careful case, may serve as an example. Gewirth argues that universal rights to freedom and well-being can be established on the basis of reason. The argument goes essentially like this: As a person who has purposes that I seek to carry out (and such are we all), I must recognize that my successful action requires that others do not interfere with my freedom and well-being. I thus claim a right against such interference. But the sufficient reason on the grounds of which I claim this right—namely, having purposes and wanting to fulfill them—holds as much for everyone else as for me. Therefore, I must rationally accept that no one's freedom and well-being should be interfered with: that everyone has rights to these.

But if I recognize that my successful action requires non-interference from others, does this as such give me a *right* against such interference? What permits my transition here to the use of concepts like "right" or "should," with their implications of universal applicability? What is to keep a Callicles or a Nietzsche from saying to themselves: "I don't want others to interfere with me, so I will do everything I can to prevent that from happening, but I certainly won't hesitate to interfere with them." They might even further say, sotto voce: "To keep others from interfering with me, I'll pretend there is a right against such interference—but I certainly don't really believe in any such thing!"

Gewirth's argument, like Kant's and like social contract theories, will thus be cogent only to a person already committed to fairness or ethicality. Hume would seem to have been correct in arguing that rationality cannot provide a basis for ethical action without my having relevant concerns or desires to begin with.

But then, cannot desire itself be the basis for ethical action? Plato and Aristotle saw the good as what we ourselves really want—with reason playing a critical role in our coming to understand what we do really want. Why was there no return to the view that morality is based on our own desires?

Some philosophers, notably Hume himself, did propose this. "Everything, which contributes to the happiness of society," Hume wrote, "recommends itself directly to our approbation and good will. . . . No man is absolutely indifferent to the happiness and misery of others." [32] We ourselves desired the good of others and the good of society, and our very wanting to contribute to these ends gave morality its basis.

As a matter of fact, the part of this concerning the happiness of society caught on. The idea that it was people's happiness that really mattered for morality, that the ethical was whatever makes for society's greatest happiness and the unethical whatever goes against it—the essence of utilitarianism—gained a wide following. But the idea that morality could be based on a person's *own* desires—that you should be ethical and contribute to the general welfare because of your own wishes—this idea won few adherents.

One reason, as we already discussed in relation to Plato and Aristotle, was that it just did not seem plausible to claim that what was ethically best was always what you most desired. Some thinkers did try to make this claim. Bishop Butler, for example, maintained that "conscience and self-love, if we understand our true happiness, always lead us the same way. Duty and interest are perfectly coincident; for the most part in this world, but entirely and in every instance if we take in the future, and the whole." [33] But he did not seem able to do without the weights of heaven and hell to come. Kant even considered it to be a kind of argument for God's existence that there was no way to guarantee a perfect relation between virtue and happiness without him. [34]

The fact is, we have conflicting desires. Not all our desires are in line with morality. We often want what it is immoral to pursue—one has only to look at the daily press for bounteous illustrations, offered up in painstaking detail. Morality cannot plausibly be identified with all our desires, only with some of them. Even when people are not misled or confused, even when they are not failing to keep what matters to them in the forefront of their minds, what they most want is not always going to be good for everyone else. In order to try to assure certain basic rights like the right not to be mugged or raped, we all fall back on the use of authority: police and prisons, if not God and hell. *Some* impositions and sanctions are necessary, at least in the world as we know it. The desires people themselves have are not always sufficient for morality.

That they are not always sufficient, however, does not mean that they never are. If the welfare of others and the ties connecting people are of any concern to you—and we believe that perhaps everyone with the exception of true psychopaths disinterestedly cares about at least some others and some social units—then authority, whether direct or internalized, is not the only basis for ethical behavior. That another's fate matters to you will mean that you yourself will want to help them; that good faith matters to you will mean that you yourself will want to avoid deceit and breaking your word. I should go beyond a minimal ethic, as we see it, not because of coercive outside forces, but because of desires I myself possess.

This view—which Plato, Aristotle, Buddha, and Confucius would all have regarded as fairly obvious—never regained much acceptance in the Western world. Since Christianity, people have tended to conceive of ethics as something opposed to desire. It is precisely in the nature of morality, as most think of it, to put something else above what we ourselves want. Though sometimes your desires might lead you in the same direction as morality would, there is nothing ethical in doing what you want. Kant even said that a beneficent action has no true moral worth when it derives from finding pleasure in the satisfaction of others, but only when, as with the cold and indifferent, it is performed without inclination and simply from duty. [35]

While not all go as far as Kant, it is generally felt that an ethical action is one performed not because of what you want but because of what you ought. To count as ethical, so it is held, an action must be based on something other than your own desires. It is our contention that this is a mistake. To be sure, not all desires are ethical to act upon. Following some would be unethical—for example, taking food away from a hungry child and eating it yourself. But does *giving* food to that child lose any right to be considered ethical because of its being something you want to do? What seems to us to matter for the ethicality of an action is not whether you do it because you want to or not, but the purposes aimed at: the nature of what you are trying to accomplish. If your action is just for your own self-interest—to eat well, to make money for buying prestige goods, to gain social recognition—there is nothing particularly ethical about it. But to try to get food to people who are hungry, to help foster children find loving homes, to work at finding effective ways to redress grievances—these seem no less ethical because achieving them will make you happy.

An activist lawyer writes, "In 1981 an old truck driver came and asked our firm's help for some 200 retirees. A Teamster pension fund had cut their benefits by nearly two-thirds.... For the next four years we lost, lost, lost, and lost, and then, home run, bottom of the ninth, we won. Everything. Suddenly, after all that losing, the case was over, and the men will now recover millions of dollars." [36] The lawyer wanted to see this wrong righted. He exults in the victory. Is his action less ethical for being based on his desire?

Plato and Aristotle had no difficulty granting moral status to actions you wanted to perform. Why does there seem to be a difficulty now? Is it essentially because the religious traditions that came after them left their imprint on the terms of analysis used by those who then sought non-religious groundings for morality? Do we have trouble seeing how an ethical action could be based on our desires because in the back of our minds there remains a legacy from the belief that "we can neither will nor do any good thing" without the help of God? [37]

The good had been banished from ourselves, and given over to the divine. As Pascal expressed it: "The 'ego' is hateful.... In a word, the 'ego' has two qualities; it is essentially wrong since it makes itself the centre of everything; it is a nuisance to others because it tries to enslave them, for each 'ego' is the enemy and would fain be the tyrant of all the rest." [38] What was moral had become precisely the renunciation of our wishes, with their inevitable self-centeredness, and attention instead to those of God.

But is the "ego" really that hateful? Was Hume not right that we have desires—among others—for the good of other people and society? In the next chapter we will present some arguments against the view that human beings are exclusively self-centered. For the moment, simply consider whether this view jibes with your own experiences, both of yourself and of others. To use an example from the Confucian scholar Mencius, over two thousand years ago, would not you—and others you know—have a sense of distress if you suddenly saw a child on the point of falling into a well? [39] Would you not want to do something about it? Does this seem plausibly understood as a reaction forced upon you by an authority's pressure? Recently a toddler was rescued by Herculean drilling efforts from a deep, extremely narrow well shaft into which she had fallen. "When Jessica was finally brought to the surface, even the burly oilfield workers who brought about the rescue were left in tears." [40] They wanted to save her and worked fifty-eight and a half hours until they did.

If we try to put all preconceptions aside, is there really any reason to think that, in order to be ethical, an action must be based on something extraneous to your wants? Rather, it seems to us that there is a basic incoherence in the whole idea that a purposive action—and everyone seems to agree that an action must be purposive if it is to be ethical—should not be based somehow on what the agent desires. How can a purposive action not aim at a wanted end?

The Christian tradition itself, ironically enough, held that being ethical was always to your own ultimate advantage, in your future life if not in this one. Somehow it was all right if divine rewards were the reasons for your actions, though they could not be motivated by earthly desires. But does it not seem, if anything, *more* ethical, if you act with fairness, generosity, and responsibility toward others because you want to contribute to a just society in which people trust and help one another, rather than because you want to go to heaven?

The idea that ethical actions cannot be based on our own wants seems to rest on confounding desire with individual advantage; what you care about, with interest in your own person. For you to have any reason at all to perform an action, there has to be desire or caring; for it to be an ethically good action, these desires must not be ones centering only on the narrow, delimited "I." We would agree that ethically good acts cannot be based on desires for personal benefit; but we would argue that they can be—and are—based on desires nevertheless.

If this were not so—if it were true that all that can make us moral is authority and its sanctions, direct or internalized—then indeed the only way for ethics to have centrality in our lives would be the authoritarian way, and the only way to protect autonomy would be minimalism. But morality's hold on us does not come solely from the coercive levers of authority. People can, because of what they themselves care about, wage legal battles to right wrongs for others despite hardship, struggle to figure out what they might do that would be useful in the world, and try to maintain commitments despite temptations to the contrary. Our own desires for the good of others and society—often insufficiently recognized due to the banishment of morality from the human sphere that took place in Western religion and left its further marks on how ethics was understood—these desires mean that there is a basis consistent with individual autonomy for much more than a minimal ethic. They do not mean, however, that such an ethic will be spontaneously or painlessly enacted.

Sharing the minimalists' commitment to autonomy, we agree with them that all you have a right to insist on from others is non-infringement. But we do not agree that non-infringement is all that you yourself should aspire to, or all that you should want to encourage in your children, or in anyone else. As we shall discuss further in the next chapter, most people—and probably all, at least if they develop under reasonably benign conditions—care about the welfare of more than their own narrow selves. On the other hand, these concerns, as Plato, Aristotle, Buddha, and Confucius knew full well, are not always clearly in the forefront of our thought. Reminding ourselves, and sometimes others, of these concerns, and considering what follows from them, is not necessarily imposition—although it can be. The distinction between imposition and the elucidation of our own deepest convictions—between social pressure and arriving at what we want to be our stance in the world—is not always an easy one to make. But it is there to be made by each of us, if we take ourselves seriously enough.

5

What the Humanists Forgot

The last chapter described how, with the developments of the Judeo-Christian tradition, ethics came to be a matter of what God wanted, not what you yourself wanted; and how human beings came to be seen as fundamentally sinful. For those whose thinking then became more secular, society and its authorities were substituted for God and Church as the sources of our goodness. This substitution left the assumed externality of ethics intact. Ethics remained something that did not originate from within but from without, and was thus inevitably tied to the use of external forces and restraints. Many then believed that there had to be forceful and extensive outside controls, whether religious or secular, and urged their routine application.

If some no longer thought it to be the authority of God that determines what is moral, they offered the authority of the social order in God's place. And if it was no longer the prospects of heaven and hell that were viewed as enforcing morality, the sanctions of society, as administered by its agents, became the moral warrantor—physical sanctions some of the time, approval and disapproval continually. "Socialization" became the scenario, whether imposed upon Freudian libido or upon behavioristic drives and reflexes. First our parents, then our teachers and other agents of socialization, according to the scenario, disapprove of us and punish us for violations of societal standards, and praise and reward us for doing what the society regards as ethical. As a result we not only come to behave more ethically, but to internalize society's standards, approving and disapproving of ourselves in terms of these standards, and passing them on when we in turn arrive at positions of authority. [1]

But what, then, of autonomy? Am I simply to let myself be imposed on in this way? Those who understand morality in socialization or social-learning terms would deny that naked imposition is really what they mean. You still have your conscience, they would say: that is what you are to follow. But my conscience seems of little help, if it in turn is nothing in its own right but an effect of the prescriptions of the social group. If my conscience merely represents the accretion of external standards that have been deposited and internalized over time, itself a product of threats and cajolings from those who have power over me, then to follow my conscience is hardly behaving autonomously either. It is still letting others shape me; indeed, behavior modifiers even use the "shaping" of behavior by outside forces as a technical term for what they aim at.

This awareness that social sanctions no less than divine prescriptions undermine personal autonomy has fueled the minimalist outlook. If autonomy comes first, then attempts at controlling people in the name of morality are not to be tolerated. The answer to such attempts, many have thought, is to insist that individuals be left to their own moral devices, free to pursue personal ends without judging one another. It is impositions as such that constitute the greatest danger to human dignity. Morality can be trusted to take care of itself, according to the minimalist outlook. Central to this line of thinking has been a humanism that rejected the assertion shared by the religious and the secular varieties of moral authoritarians alike—that human beings have little or no good within themselves.

Rousseau was a particularly important source of inspiration for this humanism; some of the neo-Freudians and especially the "third force" or humanistic psychologists ("third force" in contrast to the first and second forces of Freud and behavior modification) are current representatives. These humanists have been committed to the primacy of autonomy and have argued for human nature as good. They are often seen as rejecting much of the Judeo-Christian tradition and returning more to the views of the ancient Greeks. As we see it, however, such imputations of descent from classical Greece have an irony. For while most modern humanists stay closer to Plato and Aristotle than seems appropriate in their tendency to neglect the darker side of human nature, they have lost sight of another part of Plato's and Aristotle's thinking about ethics that seems crucially important. This is the point that ethical conduct does not just spontaneously happen but requires thought and discipline, needs to be worked at.

We do not always automatically do what is best if we are only uncoerced. Even when an ethical action is entirely in line with what we really most want, other desires often capture us. And being spontaneous and expressing our feelings can take us along ways we regret and wish we could cancel. The good, once wanted, does not flow simply from an absence of external pressure. It takes consciousness-raising and effort; it calls for dedication to keeping the broader implications of what we do in the forefront of our minds, and acting accordingly. In short, it calls for more than the ethical minimalism it receives from contemporary humanists.

For the raising of consciousness, whatever the "re-education" camp travesties perpetrated in its name, meant in its original sense not conformity to influence but helping people to see the implications of what they themselves care about. Since there *is* good in human nature—or so we will argue in the next section—making ethics significant to us need not be a matter of authorities' imposing external regulations and restraints that will pound our biology into a moral shape. It can result from our own autonomous wishes, the urgings of our own genetic equipment. At the same time, the discerning of what we really want, and the acting upon it, will take struggle within ourselves—a quest in which others can instruct without "training" us, can enlighten without "socializing" us. We can try to concentrate on what most matters to us; we can seek guidance and invite reminders.

This is not, however, the direction that the main strands of humanism since Christianity have taken. Rather, they have come to oppose anything other than individual spontaneity and self-expression. Trouble for both society and the individual came to be seen as the result of interference with the organism, whose autonomy is paramount. What seems to have happened is that the idea of ethics as external, as coming from outside ourselves, had become too firmly entrenched. Ironically, this part of Christianity was kept even by those secularists who now discarded the idea of human sinfulness. If ethics meant the imposition of external pressures, then the only way to preserve autonomy was a minimal ethic. With their faith in letting our natural goodness unfold, what the humanists have typically tried to promote is untrammeled expression of presumptively wholesome selves; any call for particular kinds of efforts constitutes an infringement on autonomy and is to be sedulously avoided.

The evolutionary biology of human nature does in fact seem to provide a built-in disposition to care about others and not only ourselves, though this disposition may readily be swamped by concern for our own welfare. This already is a controversial claim, and you will want to consider carefully our grounds for making it in what comes. It implies that there is goodness within us to start with, which contests the moral authoritarians in their argument that becoming good requires yielding our autonomy to divine or secular authority. But what we are saying also is different from the humanists' view that by nature we are always good and the source of all evil is coercion, with the consequent favoring of a minimal ethic that asks of us only that we not interfere with one another in the pursuit of our individual ends.

Our viewpoint does not make coercion any better, but it does imply that going beyond a minimal ethic need not be a matter of coercion. Such morality takes effort and cultivation, but rather than violating our autonomous wishes, it may be the best way to satisfy them—just as intensive work and practice on a sport or musical instrument may further what we ourselves really want.

The Good in Our Genes

Following upon the Christian tradition and exacerbated by capitalism, with their master assumptions of sinfulness and greed, respectively, the majority view of human nature in Western culture of our time has not been very positive. The picture was not improved by the efforts made in Freudian and behavioristic psychological circles to debunk as naive and unscientific the idea that our nature may include altruistic or ethical tendencies. Science was thought to invalidate such romanticism. The source of morality, now for science as well as for religion, lay outside us.

"It is in keeping with the course of human development that external coercion gradually becomes internalized," said Freud. "Every child presents this process of transformation to us; only by that means does it become a moral and social being." [2] (Ironically enough, this continuation of the Western religious view of the external source of morality is presented in a paper largely devoted to claiming the illusoriness of religion.) The Freudian position is echoed in what is largely taken for granted in behavioristic accounts of moral development. As one academic psychologist in the widely influential "social learning" tradition recently put it, "to behave morally is to have internalized the controls on behavior that inhibit harmful acts and facilitate beneficent acts (acts that promote the well-being of others)." [3]

In the last few years, however, an increasing number of psychologists have been recognizing that this socialization or internalization view has just been assumed, rather than grounded in evidence or logic, and that observations of human young are not in line with it. [4] Researchers have amassed large numbers of examples of friendliness, of spontaneous sharing, of sympathy and compassion, among very young children. Thus, young children often show reactions to distress in others that are strongly suggestive of the kind of sympathy with others' feelings that Hume thought of as the natural basis of ethics, as for example an eleven-month-old girl, who, upon seeing another child fall and cry, puts her thumb in her mouth and buries her head in her mother's lap. [5]

What children do is often hard not to see as attempting to provide comfort or help—even well before they are capable of understanding the difference between what provides comfort to others and to themselves when in similarly straitened circumstances. For example, one boy a little over a year old had a security blanket which he would suck when in distress. One day when he had upset his mother to the point that she herself was crying, he ran for his security blanket and tried to stuff it into her mouth. [6] Another boy, a two-year-old, when he saw a child get his finger caught in a tin box and begin to cry, immediately put his own finger into that child's mouth. [7]

A very young child can show quite strong desires to relieve another's distress. A little girl, whose parents were away and would be gone for two weeks, was visiting a twenty-month-old boy. When she was about to leave, she began to cry about her parents' absence. The boy looked sad and then offered her his teddy bear, to which he was very attached, to take home. Although his parents tried to make him realize that he would miss the bear, he insisted that she take it with her. [8]

A great deal of protectiveness and empathy is often shown by toddlers to their younger brothers or sisters. [9] Some of this is of course what the parents urge and hope for, but it also often takes the form of defending the young sibling specifically against a parent's scolding or punishing. One mother reports that when she scolds a toddler's little sister, he says, "Oh, you are mean. She doesn't understand," and goes to her and comforts her. Another reports being told by a toddler, "You mustn't do that to Alan; he's only a baby." [10] A somewhat older child is described as regularly going to his sister to comfort her when she is crying, even when expressly forbidden to do so. [11]

Recent work has undertaken to document occurrences of these kinds in a systematic fashion. Mothers of twelve- to eighteen-month-old toddlers were trained to make on-the-spot tape recordings at home, narrating in detail incidents where their child was exposed to others' distress, such as the child's brother's falling from a high chair. These naturalistic observational diaries were kept over a nine-month period. Responses suggesting some kind of empathic or helpful concern were often found in these circumstances. Responses of callousness or aggression toward the victim were about half as likely. [12]

Negative reactions to signs of distress in others even appear at the very beginning of life: newborns are likely to cry in response to the cry of another. [13] One study suggests that the otherness is critical here: a recording of their own previous crying or of a synthetic sound did not produce this effect. And infants three months old and probably even appreciably younger appear disturbed when their mothers act in a depressed manner. [14]

These examples do not readily fit the picture that beneficent action must derive from external coercion, or that it is only by means of internalization of controls that the child will "become a moral and social being." What they seem to suggest is an inherent sociality and a resonance in the very young individual for troubles outside his or her own skin. Perhaps such resonance only reflects distress over present or anticipated troubles of one's own—some social science cynics have conjectured as much—or defiance of one's parents. Especially in view of the young ages involved, however, that at least some of these observations may show rudimentary forms of inborn social concern at work seems worthy of consideration.

But could concern for others really be based on something that is within us from the start? Could it possibly derive from our biological constitution? What is biological, what is physical, what is animal-like, often has strong negative associations—as may be seen in the very word "beastliness" itself. "Nature red in tooth and claw" may seem like a thoroughly implausible basis for admirable human qualities. Doesn't evolution itself—the "survival of the fittest"—imply egoism and competition, rather than cooperation and helpfulness?

While that was an early interpretation of evolution which made its way into popular circles, one which certainly influenced Freud and other psychologists, not to mention capitalistic economists, it was quickly laid to rest among biologists themselves—that is, until recently. Until the last twenty years or so, most biologists would have denied that evolution implies an absence of helpfulness. Natural history may be full of ways in which animals prey upon and kill one another, but it is also full of ways they aid each other. Not only do parents of large numbers of different kinds of species expend great effort in the care, feeding, and protection of their young, but there can be intricate patterns of parental cooperation in this caretaking. [15] Birds and ground squirrels give alarm calls that warn others of an approaching danger; Thomson's gazelles protect others of their group by leaping in front of a predator. Certain kinds of bees sting potential robbers of their colonies' honey, in the process tearing out vital parts of their own bodies and then dying. Dolphins rescue one another and also members of other species when they are injured. [16]

Nonetheless, the pessimism taken as the initial popular reaction to Darwinism has made a more sophisticated comeback. Recently some biologists have lent their voices to the idea that helpfulness is not likely to have evolved among humans, and ethics must be imposed by society. One has written, "Let us try to *teach* generosity and altruism, because we are born selfish." [17] Another argues that, "if we ever hope to attain real altruism in human behavior, unalloyed by selfish concerns, we had better look to society to drum it into us, because there seems no other way it can get there." [18] And a social scientist, taking current biology as showing "that pure altruism, uncontaminated by evolutionary self-interest, cannot possibly evolve," finds renewed support for Freud in this. [19]

All biologists actually recognize that such tendencies of animals to help one another as we saw in the above examples have evolved by natural selection. When they talk about "altruism" and "selfishness"—though they sometimes seem to forget this—they are usually not thinking, as non-biologists would be, in terms of the interests of the individual, but in terms of preserving the individual's genes. Any evolved tendency, according to the theory of evolution, must further the propagation of the genes of the organism. The tendency's selective advantage is what it does for the genes. Often, cooperation with or aid to other organisms will be favored. An obvious example is parental care of offspring. Aid to other relatives can similarly contribute to the perpetuation of the organism's own genes. This is the basis, for instance, of such self-sacrificial behavior as that of the bees who kill themselves in the process of saving the honey for the rest of their group. These bees themselves are incapable of having offspring, but are genetically closely related to the other members of their colonies. Improving relatives' chances to pass on their genes makes genetic sense for them.

And it is not only aid to actual relatives that is rendered likely on the basis of the genetic similarities among kin. In the course of evolution many animals, including our own ancestors, probably could not recognize their offspring or other kin as such. Other factors, such as the familiarity that comes from spatial proximity, likely became proxies for kinship per se. An animal in the vicinity was more likely to share your genes than one further away. Being nearby, being familiar (note the lexical relation to the word "family"), or being similar in some way to you or to other familiar animals have probably often served as "cues" to relatedness. [20] In other words, in the animal world an individual who is unrelated to another may often be treated "like a brother." Familiarity breeds not contempt but adoption.

Adopted kinship on the basis of proximity and thus familiarity may even cross species lines. A stray Irish setter, for example, three weeks after being adopted by a family, was left in a parked car with a sleeping two-year-old while the parents walked into a car dealer's showroom. The old car suddenly caught fire and the husband, watching from the showroom, saw the dog jump out, put his paws up near the rear window, reach his head in through the smoke, and yank the frightened little girl out by her coat collar, then nudging her away as the car quickly was consumed by flames. Apparently, the dog had adopted the family, too. Both dog and child suffered slight injuries. [21] While, as we see here, use of kinship proxies like familiarity is not an infallible guide to relatedness, familiarity can be a sufficiently accurate cue that using it will give one's genes an evolutionary edge and therefore be favored.

It is clear, thus, that biologists are speaking loosely when they say that we are born selfish. If anything can be said to be selfish by nature, it is the gene, not the individual. A selfish gene can be—and often is—served by an unselfish individual. There was a real problem, however, behind the recent skepticism about the evolutionary viability of altruism. This is the problem of "free riders."

Suppose that, in some population, there is a general tendency towards help-giving. This will usually mean at least some small degree of cost to the individual helper, in terms of risk or loss or at least expenditure of effort and energy. For example, suppose a group of mostly unrelated birds tend to issue warning calls when they see a predator approaching, enabling all to try to protect themselves but drawing some attention to the warner. A mutation might lead to an individual who does not have this tendency. Such an individual would be a "free rider": it would benefit from the help (warnings) just as much as the helpers (warners), while not incurring any loss or risk to itself. The free rider would be more likely to survive, as would its progeny. Ultimately, whatever genes were involved in the help-giving would lose out. Or at best, they would be perpetuated only if the individual had some way to ensure that help would be reciprocated. General help-giving without assurance of quid-pro-quo return would thus disappear across subsequent generations—such help-giving would not be an "evolutionarily stable strategy."

Might not the genes associated with help-giving still be perpetuated because of the benefits to the group? Of two comparably sized groups, one containing a greater number of helpful individuals would seem more likely to survive than one with fewer. Why would not this suffice to promote the natural selection of helpfulness? This is actually how most biologists had thought till about twenty years ago. Behavior like alarm calls had been explained in terms of benefits to the group or species. Some biologists have indeed continued to think this way. Many, however, once aware of the free rider problem, came to believe that under most actual circumstances there would not be enough evolutionary time for such a group effect to take place. That is, the free riders would gain faster than their groups would lose, and helpfulness would not be able to maintain itself.

Some tendencies to helpfulness, such as alarm calls themselves, were of course still recognized as having evolved through natural selection, but they were usually explained in terms of close kinship among the individuals in question. For human beings, many biologists now thought such evolution to be unlikely.[22] Human gene preservation might still serve to promote aid to offspring and a few close relatives. But otherwise, the only built-in basis for giving aid was being able to anticipate getting it back. Helpfulness in humans would occur—so these biologists thought—only if reciprocation could be counted on and enforced; there could be no such thing as the evolution of disinterested concern for others. With the exception of kin, we—not only our genes—*were* born selfish after all.

This conclusion seems, however, to have been reached much too quickly. There is not only the point that in our evolutionary history kinship was probably not recognized as such but rather on the basis of imperfect cues like proximity and familiarity, which would suggest that at the very least, besides exempting kin from our pure selfishness, associates should also be exempted. More significantly, it has become clear that one cannot legitimately infer from the free rider problem that we are born bereft of general helpful tendencies. Two very recent lines of work show quite different and mutually compatible ways in which such altruistic tendencies may well have evolved and remained stable despite the possibility of free riders.

One of these has to do with animals' typical life cycles. The biologist David Sloan Wilson [23] has pointed out that in many species most face-to-face interactions take place within relatively small groups. Genetic mixing, however, takes place among a much larger population. Often when the young mature they tend to disperse, and to choose their mates from among a much larger set than those with whom they have been interacting for most of their lives. Genetic competition will occur within this larger set, but tendencies to helpfulness will have their major effects in the smaller subsets in which there is extended interaction. While the particulars on such emigration for breeding will vary from species to species, a growing ethological literature attests to this outbreeding in a variety of species, including, among others, chimpanzees, monkeys, and baboons. [24]

Such a sequence means that free riders would not keep tendencies to helpfulness from being evolutionarily stable. Animals in groups whose members interact over an appreciable period of time should be the better off the greater the proportion of helpful members and the smaller the proportion of free riders. Suppose, for example, helpers share food resources while free riders take all they can get for themselves. All the members of a group, free riders as well as helpers, will be the better off the less that free riders predominate in that group. Every member of a group in which there are few free riders will have been the beneficiary of food sharing from many others, rendering each member of such a group more fit as a result. But groups like that will of necessity be sending forth relatively few free riders into the larger population in which genetic competition takes place. Free riders entering that genetic fray are more likely to come from groups that contained more of them to begin with, and thus to be disadvantaged by the lesser food resources they received from their peers. They may have looked good in their original frog pond, but once they jump into the bigger one for breeding, it is a new ball game. Free riding may be advantageous for individuals, but as an evolutionary strategy it has its problems.

David Sloan Wilson presents mathematical arguments to show that with the kind of life cycle described, helpful tendencies should be naturally selected for so long as the proportions of helpful members differ in the different groups of interactors. If there were no variation at all—if the groups of interactors all had the same proportions of helpers—then such tendencies would not be expected to win out. There would be nothing to overcome the greater benefit of helpfulness to the free riders than to the helpers, and thus the genes promoting help-giving would not be expected to be propagated.

But variation there will be. Even if helpers and non-helpers were merely assigned on a random basis to the groups of interactors, variation in proportions would result, so that natural selection should already occur for such tendencies to give aid as were not ultimately sacrificial in terms of the helper's own genes. Though free riders within the group of interactors would benefit more than the helping individuals, helpfulness would be selected for in the population as a whole. Further, Wilson offers reasons to expect that helpers and non-helpers would typically not just be randomly distributed to the groups, but that helpers would be more likely to be found with other helpers, and non-helpers with other non-helpers, enhancing thereby the variation in proportions. To the extent this trend toward like's congregating with like was the case, there should even be natural selection for aid-giving tendencies involving increasing degrees of genetic self-sacrifice.

Does David Sloan Wilson's conception apply to humans? Those of us with grown children are often sadly aware of the tendency to dispersal with maturity. It certainly seems true that most interactions as young humans develop take place in relatively small groups, and that mates tend to be chosen from within much larger ones—out-breeding is the norm. (It has even been reported that Israeli kibbutz children, reared communally, seek mates from outside the kibbutz despite the trouble of doing so. [25]) And this contrast may even have been more extreme earlier in our evolutionary history than it is today, since, for better or worse, groups of extended primary interaction are themselves now more dispersed than they once were. A tendency to care about others and be helpful to them that has nothing to do with kinship may thus well have developed in our species in the way Wilson describes. All it takes is out-breeding, and out-breeding tends to occur.

The work of Robert Axelrod and William Hamilton [26] describes another way in which at least an initial tendency towards helpfulness may have evolved among humans, and remained stable. The free rider problem is overcome here not, as with David Sloan Wilson, by the nature of living arrangements, but by the possibility of reciprocation. If interacting individuals are capable of recognizing one another and of remembering their most recent interactions, they can be helpful or cooperative when they first meet another, without prior assurance of return, but discontinue this if the other does not behave similarly. Where repeated interaction occurs among the same individuals, continued free riding will not be possible. Free riders will get what they deserve.

This line of work, begun by the political scientist Robert Axelrod, originally had nothing to do with the evolutionary biology of altruism at all. Axelrod was interested in the idea that even if there were no common interests or concern for others among human individuals, the possibility of reciprocation means that there would still often be a reason for people to help each other. He wanted to explore the conditions under which this was the case. In terms strictly of the individual's own interests, when does it "pay" to help or cooperate?

Axelrod made use of a well-known formalization of the problem of mutual helpfulness or cooperation known as the "Prisoner's Dilemma." Suppose the authorities apprehend two men, almost certain that they have committed a crime together, but with insufficient evidence to convict them on anything but very minor charges. Each man is given the opportunity to turn state's evidence, and told that if he confesses but the other does not, he will be let off free while the other will be convicted. That is to say, each is invited to fink on the other. If both confess, leniency will be urged in sentencing. If neither confesses, both emerge with

What the Humanists Forgot

minor penalties. The "game" is choosing whether to be a fink and confess or maintain solidarity with your associate. Communication with the other player is not permitted, of course. You will have a better personal outcome if you confess than if you don't, whether the other player confesses or not. (If the other confesses too, your sentence will still be more lenient than if you hadn't confessed; if the other does not confess, you are off scot-free.) But if both of you confess, you are both worse off than if you cooperate with each other and neither of you confesses.

The crux of the approach is that the game can be played repeatedly. Numerical points—think of them as redeemable chips—can be assigned to the different outcomes (say, each player is awarded four points if both maintain solidarity and cooperate with each other but two points if both are finks, while if one cooperates and the other finks, the cooperator gets no points and the fink gets six), with a running total kept of each player's score. If the players could talk to each other, they obviously could agree to cooperate, but this is not allowed. Each one knows only what choices the other has made in previous cycles of the game. What strategies will be the winning ones to follow in such a game? If you cooperate, the other player may take advantage of you. But if the strategy both of you adopt is never to cooperate, neither of you will do as well as if the two of you had cooperated. In terms strictly of your own interests, what is best for you to do? This was Axelrod's question.

He proceeded to try to answer it in a novel way: by holding an unusual sort of competition among experts in decision games and strategies from all sorts of different fields of study, including political science, economics, mathematics, and psychology. Such experts were invited to submit computer programs—formalized strategies—for a Prisoner's Dilemma tournament. Each of the programs submitted was then run in the computer against each of the others as well as against a purely random one.

The strategy that came out on top was to start with cooperation and then do whatever the other player did the time before: we might call it "reciprocal cooperation." Other strategies that did well too—substantially better than all the rest—similarly started with cooperation and were never the first not to cooperate. A second, larger tournament found the same results, and analyses indicated that what made the winning strategy so successful was the combination of two things: (1) always cooperating unless the other failed to, and (2) retaliating when the other did not cooperate but being "forgiving"—immediately cooperating again when the other did likewise. (While the strategy was dubbed "tit for tat" as a nickname, that appellation seems insufficiently to reflect its bias favoring benevolence.)

"That is all well and good," you may be thinking—"so it pays to be cooperative and forgiving. But what does this have to do with the evolution of concern for others?" The point is that when interacting individuals are able to recognize one another and to remember their previous encounters, whether they cooperate or not can be viewed as a kind of repeated Prisoner's Dilemma game. And if it pays to be cooperative and forgiving, then perhaps we have evolved with the kind of concern for others that would make us likely to act those ways. The chips amassed by users of the winning strategy may be redeemable in the coin of evolutionary advantage. Dispositions that would lead us to risk cooperation may make genetic sense.

This seems in fact quite probable, in view of a paper by Axelrod and the evolutionary biologist William Hamilton [27] that won a prize from the American Association for the Advancement of Science. [28] They show mathematically that if you have a population of individuals who start with help or cooperation and then do what the other did the time before, no other strategy for how to treat another can gain genetic ascendancy—provided only that interactions between individuals are sufficiently likely to continue. In other words, the first thing they demonstrate is that reciprocal cooperation is an evolutionarily stable strategy.

But showing that is not enough. Never to help or cooperate is also an evolutionarily stable strategy, and it is a simpler one. In a population of non-cooperators, an individual attempting any other strategy would lose out, since whenever this individual cooperated, the non-cooperator would have the advantage, and otherwise—when neither cooperated—they would be tied. How, then, could a different strategy ever take hold in the first place? How could a built-in bias toward optimism about others ever make evolutionary headway against one favoring pessimism?

Starting with help or cooperation and then doing what the other did the previous time could gain a foothold in a population of non-cooperators, Axelrod and Hamilton show, in either of two ways: through the genetic relatedness of the interacting individuals or through clustering. Take each of these in turn. Once there is a tendency to cooperate with kin—which will be beneficial to the cooperators' own genes—cooperation itself can serve as a cue to relatedness. When an individual cooperates with another but does not receive cooperation in return, the other would be classified as non-kin and cooperation would be discontinued. But if cooperation is received in return, the other would be treated as kin and cooperation would continue. Cooperation could in this way spread among individuals with less and less relatedness, and ultimately no relatedness at all. Perhaps it is the source of power behind the ethical metaphors that call strangers our brothers and sisters. To act like kin is to become kin.

Clustering could do the job also. If, in a population of non-cooperators there is only a small cluster of a few individuals, not necessarily related, who interact frequently with one another, each of whom follows the strategy of starting with help or cooperation and then reciprocating, they will fare better than everyone else. A small cluster of reciprocal cooperators could, with their improved chances of survival, thus "take over" a population of non-cooperators. The reverse, it is important to note, is not the case: a cluster of non-cooperators interacting frequently with each other in a population of reciprocal cooperators will fare less well, not better, than everyone else. The evolutionary consequences of their perfidy to one another would give a moralist some satisfaction.

To start with help or cooperation and then do whatever the other did the time before is thus an interactive strategy that, in Axelrod and Hamilton's words, "can get started in a predominantly noncooperative world, can thrive in a variegated environment, and can defend itself once fully established." [29] This is another way, therefore, in which a human tendency towards helpfulness and concern for others—at least until they alienate us by their own actions—may have established itself through evolution. What with kinship and proxies for kinship, dispersal with maturity, and reciprocal cooperation—all of which are likely to be operating together—it seems clear that the free rider problem does not mean that we must be "born selfish." It seems far more probable, in terms of biological considerations as well as observations of babies and young children, that we are born with a tendency towards concern for others, and that those others include not only our kin.

If there *is* good in our genes, as these considerations suggest, then there is no reason to doubt that what we really want, quite apart from the impositions of religious or secular authority, can include others' welfare. The inclinations that run deepest within us may include tendencies to benefit even those who are not tied to us by kinship. Autonomy in pursuit of our wants will not necessarily result in the reign of sheer self-interest, as the authoritarians believe. But will it as a matter of course eventuate in our attending to others, can it be trusted automatically to look after whatever moral concerns we may genuinely have—as current humanistic pronouncements seem to aver?

The Insufficiency of Spontaneous Goodness

Plato and Aristotle thus may have been right after all in their intuitions that human nature contains moral goodness—even if they were wrong in believing that our real desires are always for the good. As we noted early in the chapter, these Greeks have in fact made a comeback in one form on the present scene—a form that, sadly enough in light of the interests of Plato and Aristotle, ends up favoring minimal ethics. There arose in therapeutic circles, largely in reaction to Freudian and behavioristic pessimism about the ultimate self-centeredness of human nature, strong countercurrents insisting, as did Plato and Aristotle, that people really care about such values as loyalty to friends, really want to be just, really seek to further their communities and the welfare of others. It was denied that the prescriptions and sanctions of authority are necessary in order to force us in moral directions. If given a supportive environment and allowed to follow our spontaneous feelings, all will be well. The problem is the prescriptions themselves.

Those whose outlooks lean in this direction—typically, "humanistic" psychotherapists and their forerunners, the neo-Freudians, along with some contemporary revisionist psychoanalysts like Heinz Kohut—see the individual's urges as under normal circumstances benign and trustworthy, not needful of chains and channelings in order for the public good to be served, and indeed as rendered unwholesome and pernicious to self and society alike by those very attempts at social imposition and constraint. They would tend to agree with Rousseau in his diagnosis of evil as due to our own meddling with one another. The trouble with man, says Rousseau, is that "he will have nothing as nature made it, not even man himself, who must learn his paces like a saddlehorse, and be shaped to his master's taste like the trees in his garden." [30]

Rousseau would be dismayed indeed to find the very metaphor of shaping that he here ridicules adopted by the modern behavior modifiers bent on managing contingencies to shape behavior toward virtue.

The rejection of prescriptions and restraints as necessary for morality became central to the beliefs of many therapists after Freud, reacting first against Freud's somber view of human nature and later against behaviorism as well. Take a neo-Freudian like Harry Stack Sullivan, founder of what came to be known as the interpersonal school of psychiatry, as an example. He agreed with Freud's position on neurosis: that neurosis is a consequence of internalizing the restraints imposed by others on our spontaneous impulses. But he disagreed with Freud's believing that what was bad in this way for the individual's mental health nevertheless coincided with what was necessary in some degree for the collectivity.

For Freud, the joint good of all required some sacrifice of what was best for the individual. Morality required succumbing to the prescriptions of the social order and making them our own. The advent of conscience consisted in our coming to self-administer these restraints by identifying with their sources. What gave us a civilization worth having exacted neurotic suffering as its price, because our impulses, if freely expressed, would be dystonic to everyone else.

Sullivan thought we were better than that. He spurned "the great social theory" that "society is the only thing that prevents everybody from tearing everybody to bits." [31] No trade-off was necessary between the impulse expression which alleviated neurosis and the inhibition of impulse which permitted civility. Other neo-Freudians agreed. Moral conduct, while important to them, would come naturally if we were free to realize our natures. We did not need to subject ourselves, in Karen Horney's terms, to a "tyranny of the shoulds"; indeed, to do so made us less, not more, moral. [32]

By the time of what became officially labeled as humanistic psychology, advice to liberate ourselves had become extreme. The self was to be trusted, and the greatest good was fidelity to that self and its development. Horney called this "self-realization." In the humanistic psychology movement, Carl Rogers, recently described as "originating and developing the now prevailing humanistic trend in psychotherapy," [33] and Abraham Maslow, often regarded as the father of humanistic psychology, urge "self-actualization" as what is crucial. You are to find and develop your authentic self—rejecting all the devious ways in which others, personally and through institutional forms, seek to influence you and prescribe what you are to do. Such acceptance and furtherance of self is what successful therapy accomplishes. The criterion a mature person should live by, according to Rogers, is whether something "make[s] him a richer, more complete, more fully developed person." [34] And Maslow tells us that one's environment should be "primarily a means to the person's self-actualizing ends." [35] While such an attitude may seem selfish, it is claimed not to be, since you cannot really benefit others if your basis for dealing with them springs from personal weakness and concealing your feelings. Without self-acceptance, your basis can only be defensive, leading to misery all around.

Do not let the environment hide you from yourself, these psychologists say, but rather make of it an instrument for your self-development. Since human beings are by nature good, morality will follow. Could such recommendations work out to the benefit of all, as is claimed? No doubt attempts to regulate us can violate our deepest convictions, and requiring ourselves to follow injunctions that we internalize can confuse and distress us by hiding what we really feel. Others can be harmed in the process, as when a piously self-sacrificing mother emotionally suffocates her child with her ministrations. This does not make putting oneself first always best for others as well, however. Even viewing concern for others as part of what is fulfilling to oneself does not mean that the greatest fulfillments of different ones of us will never conflict.

A mother influenced by the ideas of humanistic psychology decided to leave her three young children to be cared for by the husband she had divorced. She went off to an Indian ashram—actually, one catering to foreigners and itself influenced by these same ideas. It even pained her that her children were exposed only to her ex-husband's values, which she detested. She wrote of leaving her children, "How could I wish for them as I did, most of all, happiness, freedom and continual growth if I didn't allow myself to have it?" [36]

But if each of us, acting to further our own selves, will not automatically benefit others, will this not at least be to the therapeutic benefit of the individual? That, of course, is what Freud believed, and why he saw a contradiction between maximum freedom from neurosis for the individual, on the one hand,

and civilization's requirements on the other. As we have seen, the psychological thinking influenced by humanism denied this contradiction, romantically asserting in the process what seems to be the erroneous claim that no real conflicts exist in what would be actualizing to different people. This left humanist sympathizers free to condemn the regulations and constraints which Freud considered necessary to society's existence. Precisely because the psychological humanists rejected the Freudian pessimism about what motivates us, however, they should also have rejected his root assumption about what promotes the mental health of the individual. *This* assumption, ironically enough, they kept.

For Freud, reduction of inhibition against spontaneous self-expression had to be viewed as therapeutic and in line with the individual's desires—so long as it did not violate reality constraints—because all we can really want, at bottom, is to gratify instincts like sex or hunger. Channelings that impose too much indirection on the slaking of those urges make personal trouble for us. We would each be better off with more spontaneity, more assertiveness in gratifying ourselves. But if, as the psychological humanists insist, our basic wants extend far beyond gratifying our bodies—if we can be committed to another person's welfare, if we can care about finding a maximally just solution to a dispute, if we can seek to interpret a composer's musical intentions faithfully on the violin—advancing such of our wants as these, some ethical, others not, may call for inhibiting and restricting the spontaneous expression of other wants of ours.

What we ourselves consider, after due deliberation and examination, to be our most important wants are not necessarily our most spontaneous wants. Further, accepting the impingements of others upon us may serve the interests of, rather than stand in the way of, our deepest wants. It may be personally disadvantageous to us to submit to the workings of a legal process but we may want to do so because of what that process signifies. Another's welfare may call for personal sacrifice—a husband's doing less than the maximum for his own career because of what would be best for his wife's career—yet we may decide we want to make the sacrifice because of what it will do for the other. We may accept the discipline and regulation entailed by a violin teacher's instruction because we recognize the teacher's stature as an authority whose demands and requirements are in the service of deepening our understanding of the music, and we want that understanding.

The psychological humanists seem to be so concerned with the undermining of autonomy by external pressure and its internalized effects that they fail to distinguish between acting on the basis of what we ourselves value, and acting in terms of what will be personally fulfilling and gratifying—which may or may not be what we most value. Personal freedom is confounded with furthering the self. For the very reason that, as the humanists contend, we may well possess wants beyond our own gratification, fulfilling these may require us to inhibit and restrain ourselves and to allow some determination from the environment. "Shoulds" are not inauthentic by definition, but may represent what, upon reflection, we find we most care about.

Autonomy does not call for the cultivation of a self unencumbered by constraints or external influence, but rather for the exercise of one's own best judgment in deciding whether to accept or reject given forms of constraint or influence. Self-determination does not require the eschewing of regulation, but that *we* decide if our own wants are furthered thereby. Responding to "shoulds" or what others want or need of us, even when personally painful, even when not our first inclination, may fit our deepest convictions. As Richard Sennett puts it, "Liberty is not happiness. It is experience of division." [37] The point is that the division within us is real.

Modern psychological humanists typically end up in a very different place from Plato and Aristotle. Most alive to the dangers of restriction on our freedom, most concerned with preventing external forces from pushing us where we would not naturally go, these humanists are confident that ethics will take care of itself if only we cultivate our spontaneity. Following Plato and Aristotle all too well in believing that humans naturally want the good, they forgot what Plato and Aristotle also knew about discipline. We may have a moral nature, but Plato and Aristotle understood that we can nevertheless be forgetful of our real interests—that we are subject to distractions and lapses, to mindlessness, to ignorance and illusion, to impulses that we ourselves upon reflection consider unworthy of us. It is not our unencumbered self but our morality that needs to be cultivated; doing so does not violate our autonomy for the very reason that morality *is* a natural part of us, albeit a part that is difficult to keep in focus.

The cultivation of morality, so obviously desirable to Plato and Aristotle, was for the psychological humanists profoundly suspect. "Shoulds" conflicted with natural self-development and suggested alien imposition. They were unnecessary because our nature was benign. But a "should" need not be a foreign implant. It may derive from real wants of our own—wants that are likely to be forgotten or neglected unless we discipline ourselves to attend to them. Our wants can be at odds rather than consistent, our natures good enough to generate strictures against or ambivalence about self-oriented goals, but not so good as to make self-oriented goals the ones to pursue in the name of ethics.

A fundamental solipsism pervades the approach of humanist sympathizers in psychology. For a psychologist like Rogers, value comes not from anything outside us, but from the valuing *reaction*, the preference, per se. The source of a thing's value is our liking of it, rather than praiseworthy properties or attributes, the attempt to define which would be viewed as restricting of our freedom. The proper agenda is for us to scrutinize our subjective feelings, our reactions of liking and disliking. The one acceptable constant is to follow them. Inward is the only place to look, once it is wanted "that value reside in the self." [38] No evil exists except infringement on autonomy and the right to put personal goals first. Morality needs no special attention as long as we minimize the prescriptions we give each other. The liberal emphasis on minimalism in ethics is the necessary result. Personal preference is my compass, no one else can tell me what to do.

Some today, while accepting the psychological humanists' emphasis on self-development and spontaneity with regard to goodness, do not insist on spontaneity overall. Discipline and regulation are acceptable to them in the service of self-furtherance, but only in that service. Recall the minimalist in chapter 2 who whips herself to study harder to win personal status and success as a lawyer. You are to accept some restraints, and even do what others ask of you, but only for the sake of your own development. For anything else, it is still an imposition—a constraint on your autonomy.

But the humanists are not the only ones who confound self-focus with autonomy. Moral authoritarians, both religious and secular, do so too, but with a different conclusion. Freud, social learning theorists, behavior modifiers, and many churches all deny the natural morality affirmed by the humanists. Without sufficient coercion and control, morality will lapse. The unconstrained individual will never act for others. Where the humanists focus on the self because they see this as necessary for autonomy, the authoritarians sacrifice autonomy because they see that sacrifice as necessary for morality—concern for others rather than self.

Both accounts coordinate autonomy with self-oriented goals. Both see anything beyond a minimal ethic as implying social imposition. The first account decries subjugation and demands minimalism; the second decries selfishness and demands that we cede our autonomy. Both accounts fail to recognize that autonomy need not mean putting the self first, and that putting others first need not mean that autonomy has been given up. Both accounts fail to recognize that we can accept guidance, reminders, discipline, regulations, on behalf of others without giving up our freedom but rather on the very grounds of that freedom—our own considered judgment.

If freedom means the rejection of constraints and external determination and the furtherance of the self, then autonomy can only be preserved with a minimalist ethic. Either autonomy and minimalism, or morality and subjugation. To many, both alternatives are appalling—the dangers inherent in each only too evident—but no way out is seen. They decry how "we seem to vacillate constantly between the extremes of self-righteous, managerial manipulation, and mindless self-indulgence. Each on its own is dangerous enough, even destructive, but together they are surely a formula for annihilation." [39] To others, the current self-focus is viewed as an inevitable and inexorable historical consequence of technological development—a necessary "breakdown of authority and a stress on self"—which is therefore to be accepted if not celebrated. [40] To still others, a focus on self is unapologetically affirmed as the antidote to enslavement. As the 1986 Presidential Address to the annual convention of the American Psychological Association put it, "self-interest is freedom of choice." [41] We have argued, however, that self-focus and freedom are distinct considerations. One does not imply the other. Calling for both is a mistake that stems from contemporary humanists' having traveled too far with the Greeks in one respect and not far enough in another. But you do not have to deny both in order to correct that mistake.

What, from this point of view, becomes of our having and carrying out roles—those obligational structures often, in the current humanist temper, understood as oppressive? Start with the original sense of the term "role": that of an actor playing a role on the stage. It should come as no surprise that Rousseau found in

stage acting not the possibility of enhanced understanding of the
character portrayed, not a deepening of appreciation for something
human, but instead the actor's debasement. Performance can be
nothing but the actor's submission to shaping by another. Roles
are in no sense goals or ideals, the pursuit of which might edify
you, only molds that will distort you. "The professional deforma-
tion that Rousseau deplores is that by engaging in impersonation
at all the actor diminishes his own existence as a person," says
Lionel Trilling. [42]

Clearly this was not the effect of acting for a nineteen-year-
old retarded woman described recently by the clinical neurologist
Oliver Sacks. She was in daily living a person of patent limitations—clumsy, slow, disorganized physically and mentally. Thera-
pies based on direct help toward amplifying her personal resources
and building skills did nothing for her. She sensed that sooner
than her therapists, whose work only served to emphasize her
clumsiness of mind and body, rather like the centipede asked to
attend to its legs. But acting in the theater transformed her—and,
becoming her life, it saved her. Playing a role gave her an
integrative pattern. On stage, her limitations were not in evidence.
She said to Sacks, "I'm like a sort of living carpet. I need a pattern,
a design, like you have on that carpet. I come apart, I unravel,
unless there's a design." [43] She is extreme, of course, but hardly
shows debasement from acting.

Roles—in the theater and out of it—can be concrete render-
ings of what can otherwise remain inchoate, elusive meanings. In
his novel *Kate Vaiden* Reynolds Price plays the role of a woman,
the heroine of the title, writing in the first person as if he were
she. [44] The result, according to one reviewer, is "a sustained feat of
female impersonation that goes beyond mimicry to a sympathetic
identification with every inflection of his heroine's highly distinc-
tive voice and every twist and turn of her erratic course." [45] Price
strives to understand this woman by approximating her in his
mind, by becoming her.

The concreteness and clarity of a role to be lived or practiced
can help you define yourself in ways you may care about but can
otherwise lose track of or neglect or fail to grasp. Take the fact
that we exist as part of a generational series, beholden to others
who in one way or another fostered us, in a position to foster still
others who will succeed us. In our culture, such a formulation has
less meaning than it might, concentrating as we do on the
perspective of separate individuals marching through life to an

inexorable loss of personhood at the end—at least on this earth. We might upon reflection prefer to envision ourselves as more enmeshed in a series, the maintaining and continuance of which matters to us, if we could hang on to the idea.

Some do, even in a culture not conducive to it, think in this other way already. Recall the student in chapter 2 who saw herself located between the great-aunt who raised her and the four neglected children on whose behalf she worked as an advocate. She wondered if helping "the children that are coming next" was a way of paying off what she owed her aunt.

A society can be more conducive than ours is to thinking of oneself as part of a series. The anthropologist Clifford Geertz describes how the Balinese, for example, while they have personal names, hardly ever use them. Instead, the names by which they address and refer to one another are names that convey one's location in the generational sequence. A couple will be known as "Mother-of" and "Father-of" their first child. Then later, as "Grandmother-of" and "Grandfather-of" their first grandchild. And if they are lucky, in due course as "Great-grandmother-of" and "Great-grandfather-of" their first great-grandchild. The focus is on the new life, and on your function in having brought it about.

It is generational continuity in particular that matters, not procreational fertility. One's standing depends not on being a father or mother of more children rather than fewer, but on becoming a "Grandfather-of" instead of a "Father-of," or a "Grandmother-of" instead of a "Mother-of." The taxonomy of naming calls attention to the continuation of the community—its perpetual regenesis. The naming usages convey and clarify people's "relation to and representation in that subclass of the population in whose hands social regenesis now most instantly lies—the oncoming cohort of prospective parents." [46]

To specify one's self in terms of functions and responsibilities for others may, as Geertz points out, seem from our society's perspective depersonalizing. Yet calling attention to one's role in social regenesis may fit some of our real desires and, by de-emphasizing what about us perishes, even be good for our mental health. The point is that the language of roles is not necessarily more superficial and that of spontaneity of feeling or impulse more basic. Expressive immediacy may seem not more real but more alien to a person. It is its own kind of convention.

Ironically, humanistic psychologists, in urging the shedding of roles and the discovery of feelings, seem guilty of misapplying to human beings certain methods drawn from the physical sciences—a charge they should find embarrassing to say the least. It is like expecting the real person to be located through something akin to analysis into the elements of chemistry or the fundamental particles of physics. [47] The discrediting of the introspective psychology practiced early in the century hinged on the way that that enterprise, by its analytic decomposition of experience, acted to destroy the reality it set out to investigate. Current humanistic psychologists may have made this same mistake.

Our greatest authenticities may take us into roles, not out of them. Consider the Balinese again. What is distinctively human to the Balinese is playing roles appropriately, Clifford Geertz tells us. These cultural performances to be carried out "comprise not the facade but the substance of things, not least the self." [48] The play's the thing, not the players. The Balinese have a word, "lek," which means something close to stage fright. "Lek" is in effect one's fear that the actor will show beneath the role one is playing.

It is like fear of the collapse of an artistic performance, say in our society the playing of a Handel sonata for recorder and harpsichord. The Balinese are telling us in effect that what matters is serving the musical form—approximating that perfection in one's human imperfection, where doing so well enough gives access to that music in its greatness. Some performance lapses can be overcome by the power of the form; but too many wrong notes on the harpsichord, too unpolished a recorder tone, too many rhythmic distortions and corrupted phrasings, and the illusion of the form collapses. The point of the Balinese outlook is that the so-called illusion is the true reality, while what can break through and destroy it—the particularities of the performers with their musical warts—is less real, less authentic. What is genuine is the form to be approximated, according to one's most educated sense as to what that form should be.

Even in the musical realm there are those in our society who demur from the above formulation, believing the idiosyncrasies of a particular artistic personality to be more authentic than idealized forms—as when the pianist Glenn Gould played the first movement of a Mozart sonata like a speeded-up, whirlwind machine, much faster than Mozart could have envisioned, the second movement much more slowly than Mozart could have intended, and with various romantic exaggerations. But we can see from musical performance what the Balinese have in mind more generally when they locate greater reality in what is performed than in the performer. May this not be how moral ideals are to be understood, and the business of trying to live up to them? Rather than covers and pretenses that ought to be peeled away, they, too, may be forms that require—and deserve—practice and work to approximate.

That we may, even more often than not, fall short in our performances of roles we undertake to play does not make hypocrisies of the roles any more than it makes a virtue of our failures to live up to them. Yet modern humanism suggests both implications. Benjamin Franklin knew better. "He was all his many roles," [49] Judith Shklar reminds us, and had no problem with "the notion that one's manner of acting one's roles measures true character." [50] To attribute greater authenticity to our lapses is to deny validity to our moral aspirations wherever internal conflict stands in their way, as if the conflict can only be artificial. The moral efforts that roles represent may be at least as real to us as whatever eventuates in our moral failures, and the roles themselves a means of helping us realize and remember this. What matters is that we be the judge, rather than accept as a prejudgment that roles can only be impositional.

6

Dealing with Differences

But can you really object to values different from your own? Is it not impossible to show that one value is better than another? And is it not the rankest disrespect to say of someone that what they are aiming at is not good, that their ends are not worthy? If we are to shun intolerance and imposition, do we not have to limit what is required by ethics to autonomy and lack of infringement? Is minimalism not what is necessary for tolerance and respect toward the different ways of different people?

Or can I escape minimalism, without at the same time seeming holier than thou, by being relativistic? If I refrain from judging what is ethical for anyone but myself, is not precisely this what gives me the freedom to *be* more than a minimalist in my ethics without appearing a bigot? When another's values clash with mine, I do not have to deny that their values possess validity—their values may be right for them, while they would be wrong for me. Can I avoid minimalism, while also avoiding intolerance, by recognizing that what is right for one of us is not necessarily what is right for the other?

Keeping moral affirmations personal so as not to impose one's beliefs on others was evident again and again in our interviews. Here is an example:

> You know, people talk a lot about how drunk they were this weekend or what they did at this party and how they can't remember, and that's fine for them, but it's not me. But most

> of those people are just, you know, they're really nice people—just something different between us....
>
> Drugs and drinking, I think there's a wrong when they're harming themselves—when the situation gets out of control because they've done it so much that they've become alcoholics or become addicted—but I don't think I'm really in a position to say right or wrong for them. You know, for me, sure, there's a—I know what's right and what's wrong for me, but I can't determine that for them.

In what follows, we will attempt to show that such efforts to maintain both tolerance and moral convictions by distinguishing between what is right for you and what is right for others run into serious problems. We will argue that this balancing act is not only ill-fated, but also unnecessary. In our view, neither respect and autonomy, nor the difficulties of justifying or reaching agreement on ethical values, in fact call either for limitations on ethics or for seeing what is ethical as different for different people. Turn first to the question of what is required for respect.

Respect and Relativism

A great many of the students we interviewed wanted to take the position that what was right for others could be different from what was right for them, and believed furthermore that such an attitude was the one they *should* have. Here, for instance, is what another said:

> I may have different ideas about what I consider to be right or wrong, but that's not to say that I can say what's right for other people. I think people have a tendency to do that—to kind of impress or place their values on someone else—and they may not necessarily—the other person may not necessarily believe those values. I think it's important that even though I may think one way, that I don't try to judge other people by my own standards because they're definitely going to be different from someone else's.

This attitude was, however, clearly not an easy one to maintain. People often had trouble trying to do so. Relativism in the name of tolerance did not sit comfortably with ethical standards. Consider the signs of strain in the following statements:

> I'd say if you are doing something that is not harming anyone else or affecting anyone else except yourself—and you know what you're doing—then that's fine. . . . There's a particular person that is having sex every night with a different person. That I think is wrong because you *are* involving all these people. Then again—maybe that's what they wanted.

> . . . Well, see, I can't come out and say "that's wrong" and "that's right." Who am I to say that? Uh, I would say I would condemn it if—I mean I'm not the type that would support someone having sex with someone different every night. I mean it's just not *healthy*. But then again, that goes against what I was saying as between two people if it doesn't affect anybody else, then. . . .

Here is a second example:

> Different things are right for different people. What is the right thing for you may not be the right thing for the next person. . . . For an example, some people see nothing wrong with going out on a weekend and getting just totally drunk, so they don't even remember what they did. That's fine for them. That doesn't bother them and as long as they stay out of trouble, you know, as long as—I mean, I can see there's something wrong with that. . . .

> With science it's—it's a fact, you know, pretty much, and with ethics it would depend on the individual. And where it would be in science if one thing is right, the other thing is wrong—although it may be shaky right now, maybe five years from now you'll find out that this was right, this is wrong—that's it—that was wrong, it will always be wrong. But with ethics it might be right in one situation—it might be wrong in another. Ten years from now it might be right in one situation—it might be wrong in another. It's—it's always going to be iffy in certain situations. . . . Well, as far as like murder or something like that, I think that there would—that would be flat out just wrong. There would be certain situations again I guess that would be, you know, that would be—just always be wrong to do. . . . If someone thought that they were doing someone a favor by killing them, that

would definitely be wrong even if they thought it was the right thing to do.... That'll contradict everything I just said.

A third student says:

> There's certain issues where I think people agree and they think the same, but overall I would say what's right for one person isn't right for another.... If you're happy with what you're doing—if you're happy cheating and if you're happy killing people then I can't form a—I'm going to get myself all mixed up, because—I mean, that sounds wrong—that *is* wrong.

Here is a fourth example:

> I have a friend who shot a policeman.... From early on I knew he'd come from like a—I guess you would say troubled family, and he was really good at football and he got a scholarship to another school, and he ended up taking ridiculously hard classes and he always had a problem with drugs and stuff. He ended up failing out of that school and then he joined the Army and was kicked out of the Army for drugs and so he went back home.... He lived with his older sister and they had some problems there and he still had—still had a gun from the Army—he'd learned how to shoot and everything. So it's a long—kind of confused story, but, you know, he was kind of feeling bad about himself and so he and his sister just had a big fight and stuff and his sister called the police and when the police came he just went crazy, or he just, you know, had an outburst—in his anger, I guess, he shot and they—whatever—they convicted him of first degree attempted murder of a policeman....
>
> I always kind of am—relativistic kind of thing, you know—if it's right for you, it's right for you, and if it's not, it's not. So, you know, there's a case where if it was right for him, it's still wrong for—it's *wrong* and it doesn't really matter what you think....

A fifth student says:

> I think cultural differences are very important and what's right for one culture should be maintained, but then again it

was right for the Nazis to aggress against the rest of the world. . . . There's another paradox.

Finally, here is a sixth student:

> . . . I've had to deal with my friends sleeping with their boyfriends. Like every single one of my friends in the past year has made this jump and it's been really difficult for me to deal with. How am I going to deal with my feelings now toward them, you know, do I think what they're doing is wrong. And what I've come to decide is that if they really think what they're doing is right and they have no qualms about it, then that's right for them even though it would be wrong for me.
>
> . . . When I was like a junior in high school and one of my good friends told me that she was sleeping with her boyfriend I was really frazzled—I didn't know what to think. I'm going, "Man, if I did this it would be so wrong"—I mean, I wouldn't be able to live with myself. . . . I was starting to think, "Well, she's not being good for this." But then I decided. . .I was feeling it's wrong for me to say what she's doing is wrong. It has to do totally with what she feels is right and wrong and that's—that's why I'm saying that what she feels or, you know, he feels, that that's their way of dealing with the world and their way, you know, of dealing with their boyfriends or girlfriends and that's fine. That's not saying that I really condone it, but I'm not saying that it's wrong for them.
>
> And it's hard for me to say, "Well, it's good for them but it's bad for me," so sometimes I think I'll get a boyfriend and I'll say, "Ok, yeah, I'd like to do that," but then I'm saying, "Nope, that's wrong for you." Then I'll go, "Well, maybe I'm deciding now that it's good." I'm worried that that's going to happen to me.

When it comes to matters they really feel strongly about, people find it hard to stick to the position that you can judge only what is right or wrong for you—that what is right or wrong for others may be quite different. The trouble is that such relativism removes much of the meaning of saying that something is right or wrong. If you have a strong conviction that something is wrong, whether it is premarital sex, getting totally drunk, murder, or

Nazi aggression, you don't want to say only that it is wrong for yourself or for those who already happen to think it is wrong. You don't want to drift on a sea of personal preferences. You want to say: "it's *wrong* and it doesn't really matter what you think." But that, of course, is something you cannot say without making judgments for others.

On the other hand, if you do stick to judging only for yourself, then you can't say someone is mistaken when they see something as acceptable which you see as wrong. This makes it hard for you to maintain your conviction of wrongness. After all, if those differing from you are not in error, if it is "just something different between us," would you be making a mistake if you changed your mind? The speaker who feared she might give in and decide that sexual behavior she had come to think was right for others—without really condoning it—would also be right for herself, provides a striking illustration of the tendency for avoiding any judgment of right and wrong for others to weaken one's own value convictions—for relativism to slide into minimalism. What you refuse to object to in others becomes hard to object to in yourself.

You cannot escape from minimalism, then, by distinguishing what is right and wrong for yourself from what is right and wrong for others, because you cannot have much passion about a right and wrong that hold only for you. Either you retain strong values and then find such relativism unacceptable, or you retain the relativism and find your values eroding as you edge toward minimalism. (The erosion can even go so far as to weaken commitment to the most minimal principles, as in occasional liberal apologetics for terrorism.)

But must we be minimalists or relativists if we are to maintain respect for others? Ironically enough, tolerance is by no means a necessary concomitant of minimalism. Minimalists are often quite *in*tolerant of people who go beyond a minimal ethic. They may hold them in contempt as suckers. And they may readily place those who do not share the ideals of the liberal ethic into a sort of double bind, in effect saying both "do what you want to do" and "express your feelings"—which may not be what the other wants to do. A number of the students with whom we spoke reported having been put down for their scruples and "inhibitions" when they behaved according to their more substantial convictions. Minimalists can be closet authoritarians.

Consider how we arrive at minimalism or relativism. These attitudes hardly seem to describe states of nature. Rather, they are attempts to finesse differences. One's first reactions to being confronted with people who do not share one's ethical values likely are to brand them as somehow lacking in virtue, or to patronize them as ignorant or deluded. Of course, for authoritarians like Allan Bloom,[1] one's first reactions remain one's last reactions. But at some point many of the rest of us question our stance as crusader or missionary, recognizing that those with different convictions are in a situation parallel to our own. We have no warrant for proclaiming ourselves right and the others wrong. We come to see the disrespect and intolerance inherent in that first attitude. Minimalism or relativism—to many of us—then seems to provide a way out.

Is this what tolerance asks of us, however? Does respect for others really require that where we have differing views, there is no right or good, or only a right or good "for you" or "for me"? To think that is to assume that we cannot respect a person with whom we disagree. It is to say criticism can only be ad hominem. But surely that is not the case.

One of our interviewees clearly saw that when you care a great deal about something, you cannot make judgments only for yourself:

> I think that even though you sit back and say what somebody else wants to do is fine, in the back of your mind you judge. And that's—I don't think that's avoidable. I think that that's inevitable, because if you feel so strong about something that you build your life around it, of course you're going to judge in the back of your mind.

He also understood that you can still treat with respect those with whom you disagree:

> You have to accept the fact, yeah, you're going to judge them—but just understand that and don't let that affect the way that you deal with them.

Do scientists who propose changes in existing theories lack respect for those theories, or for the people who developed them? On the contrary, they would hardly be in a position to propose those changes if they had not respected the previous work enough to study it, ponder it, and carefully consider what might be wrong with it. We have all of us had the experience of thinking someone is wrong without believing they must be evil or dumb. There are "good errors": errors that make sense in terms of extant knowledge or available information. (After all, we are sometimes wrong ourselves.) And, as is well known by anyone who has been around philosophers for any length of time, some people much *prefer* that you take issue with them than that you simply accept what they are saying. Taking issue suggests you are really thinking about it. Mere acceptance suggests a lack of processing—what to some is the supreme insult of not caring enough to pay discriminating attention.

Respect does not call for an absence of disagreement, for the papering over of differences. Rather, it calls for taking seriously what the other thinks—for recognizing that they might be right and you might be wrong, and that you may be able to learn from them. By avoiding disagreement with someone whose values differ from yours—by simply accepting their values as right for them though not for you—are you not in fact avoiding really considering those values? It seems far more respectful to enter into what the contemporary German philosopher Hans-Georg Gadamer calls a "true conversation," in which "one opens oneself to the other, really gives weight to his point of view, and puts oneself in the other's place so as to understand him—not as an individual, but what he is saying. What is to be grasped is the substantive merit of his opinion, so we can come to see eye to eye on the matter. Thus we do not relate the other's opinion to his individuality, but back to our own views and opinions." [2]

We do not, in other words, adopt a therapeutic attitude to what the other is saying: the attitude that would refrain from judging in the name of accepting the other "as an individual." The point is not that one should recognize the other's right to self-expression, or acknowledge what they are saying as personal biography. For deeming a view to be "right for them" is to imply that there is nothing to consider *about* the view—that it is merely to be acknowledged as a valuing reaction, on a level with any other valuing reaction. What Gadamer here rejects, then, is the legacy of the psychological humanism treated in chapter 5.

The idea of coming to agree on ethical issues may seem a hopeless mirage; we will turn to that question in a moment. What we hope to have established at this point is that tolerance and respect do not require us to refrain from disagreement, or to accept views people hold that are different from our own as right for them though not for ourselves. To judge and criticize another's views in the spirit of Gadamerian conversation is to accord them much more respect than to dismiss them *as* views with non-judgmental, therapeutic acceptance. We need to remain open to the possibility of our own error, and to avoid imposing our own views. But it is not necessary, for the sake of tolerance and respect, to avoid the possibility of disagreement. Indeed, it is only when we "relate the other's opinion...back to our own views and opinions" that we grant others the respect of taking their position seriously.

Can Ethical Beliefs Be Justified?

"All right," you may want to say at this point. "Maybe relativism or minimalism is not required for respect and tolerance. But so what? Don't you have to settle for something like that anyway? Isn't any other expectation just another one of those romantic illusions for which you were faulting the current humanists?"

Apart, perhaps, from minimal principles such as not—noticeably, anyway—harming others, ethical views are widely held to be a function of accidental factors like where you were born and brought up, and particular experiences you have had. They are not regarded as beliefs you can really justify. It is generally not expected that people will be able to resolve ethical disagreements by rational processes, unless they agree on fundamentals to begin with. Anything like Gadamerian conversation, however nice in principle, is thought doomed to failure in practice.

Indeed, the ultimate unjustifiability of ethical positions appears almost as a truism these days. Even recent efforts to combat moral disarray by showing that ethics is not subjective fail to question it. The political philosopher James Fishkin, for example, is much concerned about the extent to which people in our culture think of ethics as subjective. As he says, "a moral ideology that is not objective—that supports claims to its own subjectivity or arbitrariness—strips itself of legitimacy and authority." [3] Questioning students about their responses to various ethical dilemmas, Fishkin found again and again that they saw moral views "as arbitrary, as a matter of mere taste or preference, as a matter of purely personal subjectivity." [4] Many of them felt forced to this position because they had come to see every moral assumption as open to question, answerable perhaps in terms of another moral assumption, but without the possibility of ever reaching any final stopping point. As one of them put it, "there is no ultimate justification or ultimate value in any one system of ethics. The value that some people place on good and the value that other people place on good can be in contradiction to one another, and there is no ultimate or absolute arbiter between the two." [5]

The purpose of Fishkin's book is to show that subjectivism is not necessary, that ethics can after all be objective—its title is *Beyond Subjective Morality*. Yet for Fishkin too there is no ultimate justifiability. Ethical judgments are based on different systems of ethics: for example, the principles of justice proposed by John Rawls, the utilitarian system maintained by Peter Singer, or—typically—more informal schemes. You can justify your belief that something should be done by showing this follows in terms of your ethical system; or an inquisitor can try to ferret out the system you are using even if you cannot verbalize it; but you cannot justify that system itself, nor could anyone else do it for you. After all, the greatest happiness for the greatest number could conflict with the requirements of justice, say, and you could not show that one or the other should take precedence.

There is no way, according to Fishkin, that adherents of one such system could rationally convince others of its correctness. He argues that ethical judgments can still be objective, in the sense that anyone making judgments on the basis of the same system would come to the same conclusion. But that the systems themselves cannot be justified seems to Fishkin inescapable. Ultimate justification for ethical beliefs is thus out of the question. People will have different ethical premises, and then there is nothing more to say.

Two other writers, the psychologists John Sabini and Maury Silver, are also concerned about the current tendency to think of rightness and wrongness as subjective. They want to show that this is a mistake born of confusion. As they point out, there are differences in views about facts as there are about values; descriptive as well as value judgments can be biased and distorted; and there are ambiguities in how to describe something as well as in how to evaluate it. Such forms of interpretive slippage do not mean that ethics must be subjective, for these are all problems encountered in science, too.

Neither, according to Sabini and Silver, does ethical subjectivism follow from the ultimate unjustifiability of moral judgments, which they again regard as unavoidable. This unjustifiability does not mean that moral evaluations are unreasoned reactions, they say. It is just that a chain of reasons "must end somewhere. You may have a reason for your evaluation, and you might even have a reason for that reason's being a reason. But you will eventually be forced to give up offering reasons." [6] Once again you are—presumably—up against the incommensurability of different systems.

Sabini and Silver see ethical judgments not only as ultimately unjustifiable, but as relative to the culture. This too, they argue, does not mean that ethics is subjective. For a given culture, once you are inside it, what is right or wrong is objective, in the sense of being something known by everyone. Take adultery. Even though the wrongness of adultery may be an arbitrary convention, true for one culture but not for another, "crosscultural variation gives us no reason to call its wrongness subjective.... The rightness or wrongness of adultery is, at least, a cultural fact. Of course, the wrongness of adultery can change. Perhaps in 1953 adultery was wrong; perhaps in 1995 it will clearly be right. And perhaps at the moment it is ambiguous, but none of this shows it is subjective either." [7] Small comfort if you are concerned about relativism or minimalism. If this is objectivity, it still pulls the rug out from under any attempt to defend a position. Adultery is left as a personal option you can blandly pursue in a culture in transition.

It is not only in relation to ethics that the problem of justification has become so acute, though it is likely here that this problem has had the greatest ramifications. Worry about it— sometimes replaced by exhilaration if not glee at the apparent absence of anchors—abounds today in literary studies, in philosophy generally, in the social sciences, and even in the natural sciences. Indeed, the idea of ultimate unjustifiability seems a hallmark of the current "postmodern" period of Western thought.

As the social philosopher Richard Bernstein has written, "Whether we focus on...rationality, truth, knowledge, reality, or norms, we seem to be confronted with incommensurable paradigms, theories, conceptual schemes, or forms of life. We have been told that it is an illusion and a deep self-deception to think that there is some overarching framework...to which we can appeal in order to understand and critically evaluate the competing claims that are made, and that we are limited to our historical context and to our own social practices." [8] According to the well-known historian of science Thomas Kuhn, whose work is often invoked in this connection, physical science itself, that bastion of reliable knowledge, rests on shifting sands. The data of today may become the misperceptions of tomorrow; theories change and replace one another without stateable rules or logic. [9]

If this can be said even of physical science, what hope can there be for ethics? Were Fishkin and Sabini and Silver wrong only in believing objectivity of any sort is possible at all? But consider the case of science a little more closely. It is not that what is true today is different from what was true yesterday (apart from actual changes in the world—the Grand Canyon was once solid rock, after all). Before Copernicus came along the earth was not stationary, though that was what most people believed then. Truth does not change—what we think of as truth changes. If truth itself were modified as new ideas became accepted, what would be the point of the scientific enterprise?

Nor is it that one theory can be justified as well as any other. There are good reasons for believing that the earth moves around the sun, even though this cannot be proven in the manner of a mathematical theorem. It is simply that justification, even in the most hard-nosed science, is a lot more uncertain, a great deal messier, than we might wish it to be.

Direct observation certainly does not suggest the earth's motion. Near the end of the sixteenth century, more than fifty years after Copernicus had published his views, it was still possible for the philosopher Jean Bodin, known for his advanced and radical ideas, for his heretical tendencies and his atheism, to write, "No one in his senses, or imbued with the slightest knowledge of physics, will ever think that the earth, heavy and unwieldy from its own weight and mass, staggers up and down around its own center and that of the sun; for at the slightest jar of the earth, we would see cities and fortresses, towns and mountains thrown down." [10] Perpetual earthly upheaval was not what Bodin witnessed, and he drew the obvious conclusion.

Many thought the idea of the earth's circling around the sun was absurd, not only because then you would expect your experience to be very different from what it was, but also because, as Aristotle had said, it seemed inherent in the nature of earth-like substance to move towards the center of the universe. People today sometimes scoff at such a notion, but it too rested on observation. Have you dropped a rock lately, or emptied a pail of water? A penchant to seek the center of the earth is suggested by observations of falling objects as they seemingly exert themselves to reach downward, and the course of uncontained liquids on the earth's surface. (According to Aristotle, the natural location toward which water tends would be a spherical shell around the core of earth-substance, water being heavy but earth heavier still.) And that the earth's center coincides with the center of the universe is suggested by the observed changes in position of sun, moon, and stars. They do seem to behave like satellites of the earth, after all. So you have matter irrevocably aiming toward the earth's core as the center of centers, and no basis for expecting it to seek any other location. The result is Bodin's earth, locked firmly in position, and supported there by evidence and inference.

The issue between an Aristotelian and a Copernican cannot be resolved simply by observation and logic. Like people with different systems of ethics, they will have trouble understanding one another, and each theory will seem wrong-headed to an adherent of the other. And again as in the case of ethics, neither will be able to *prove* that their position is correct, in the sense that it could then no longer be subject to question, and could never be shown wrong. But this is not to say that belief in the earth's motion around the sun is not justified!

Such a heliocentric idea ultimately permitted the apparently irregular motion of the planets to be explained without needing ad hoc kinds of special assumptions (though Copernicus himself still needed them for a precise account). "In Copernicus' system the major irregularities of the planetary motions are only apparent. Viewed from a moving earth a planet that in fact moved regularly would appear to move irregularly." [11] The idea came to seem less counter-intuitive once there had been some changes in the understanding of motion and falling objects. And, especially after the telescope had been invented, it was much more compatible with further observations than the earth's being the stable center of the universe. Indistinguishable to the naked eye, the phases of Venus, for example, turned out upon telescopic inspection to vary in conformity with the heliocentric expectation.

No observations were by themselves definitive. You could even doubt, as some did early on, that the phenomena made visible by the telescope were real, rather than being caused by the telescope itself. [12] But eventually it became clear to all concerned that accepting the earth's status as one of the planets moving around the sun made possible a much simpler and more coherent explanation of experience. A hundred years after Bodin wrote, it would have been very hard to argue that belief in the earth's motion was not justified.

Scientific beliefs can be justified, then, even though there are no unquestionable foundations and no permanent and unchanging rules of inference. It may be difficult, but it is not impossible, for people operating within incommensurable paradigms or theories to come to understand one another and engage in rational discourse. They may even come to change their minds—not arbitrarily, not due to suggestion, not against their better judgment—but precisely *because* of their better judgment. One can become convinced by the other's arguments. Kuhn himself, less than happy about some of the uses to which his views have been put, insists he never meant that "the proponents of incommensurable theories cannot communicate with each other at all," that "in a debate over theory-choice there can be no recourse to *good* reasons," or that theories "must be chosen for reasons that are ultimately personal and subjective." [13]

The justifiability of the beliefs scientists hold means that science has a kind of objectivity that goes well beyond the sorts Fishkin and Sabini and Silver discuss. There is no certainty, and what today is clearly the best available theory may be assigned to the junk heap tomorrow. But a scientific judgment is not objective merely in the sense that it would be made by anyone on the basis of the same theory, as Fishkin proposes for ethical judgments; or in the sense that it is based on something known by everyone within a certain group, parallel to what Sabini and Silver propose. A scientific judgment is objective in the sense that it is not just a function of personal or group preferences, nor of arbitrary or contingent happenstances, but of a concerted effort toward finding what is the most justified belief. This does not mean that everything said in the name of science is the most justifiable assertion that could be made. After all, scientists are imperfect like the rest of us. That is the aim, however, and the effort.

You may be ready to grant this for science—or at least willing, if pressed. It is embarrassing for us to gorge ourselves so on the fruits of Western technology without seeming ingrates if we grant less. But what does this do for ethics? Is not ethics on very different ground? We believe that despite the rampant relativism of people's ways of talking about ethics, despite the ubiquity of phrases like "right for me," an objectivity of a very similar kind is implicit in the meaning of ethical language.

Earlier in this chapter we saw how hard it is to stick to relativism if you really care about something. Talk about what one should or should not do tends to be passionate. It is hard to square such talk with the disclaimer of its expressing no more than an arbitrary reaction, a feeling that you just happen to have because of certain factors peculiar to yourself and others of like mind, such as where or according to what ethical system you were raised.

Indeed, if you really are just expressing arbitrary preferences when you use ethical language, you are at best being misleading with your rhetoric of good and bad, and quite possibly being deceptive. To condemn something or say it is bad is to give your utterance a kind of status and force it would not have if you just said that you or your group do not like it. The philosopher Alasdair MacIntyre points out that this prestige derives from the fact that terms like "bad" imply an appeal to an objective and impersonal standard.[14] If you *are* doing no more than expressing preferences, the use of ethical language would seem to be a sham—one that is, in fact, often employed for the purpose of imposing those preferences on somebody else.

Can there be objectivity to ethical judgments beyond their relationship to a system, as for Fishkin, or a group, as for Sabini and Silver? MacIntyre himself has sometimes seemed to think that what objectivity there is to ethics derives from the subordination of the individual to certain kinds of group traditions. But—quite apart from the point that if this were true, it would vitiate all hope of autonomy in ethics—any such "objectivity" is less than what seems implied when we use ethical terms. When we say something is wrong, we don't seem to mean only that our particular group or system or tradition or child-rearing history leads us to condemn it. Use of ethical language, we submit, is misleading so long as it rests on a contingent basis—on what could just as well have been otherwise. The meaning of ethical judgments is a claim to more than that. It is a promissory note that, in principle at least, pledges a non-arbitrary backing.

This is not to say that actions do not have to be judged differently where there are different traditions. It makes a great difference, for example, if marrying a second wife takes place among us or among the !Kung, where a bridegroom makes no commitment to the bride that she will be the only one. But traditions themselves, or at least the vast majority of traditions, are not arbitrary either. Although many fear that once we allow ourselves to evaluate the practices of different groups, there will be no alternative to ethnocentrism—to using the standards of our own group as criterial—just because a certain practice is customary or accepted in a given society does not necessarily mean that it should be. We can turn against social practices for moral cause even if we grew up with them.

Perhaps it would really be better if no men had two wives. Or perhaps not. Perhaps the case is more compelling that it would be better if the Ilongot did not engage in head-hunting as a way of proving their manhood. There are other ways. Or if the antebellum South had not engaged in slavery as an economic arrangement. There are other economic arrangements. You may or may not regard such questions as easily answerable, but the point is that you can make sense of them, and indeed need to consider them even in order to evaluate actions done within a given group. You cannot judge an antebellum Southerner's purchasing of a slave or helping a slave to escape without taking into account that slavery was an accepted practice, and evaluating that practice.

But by what standard can we evaluate the practices of different traditions? How can we condemn or justify practices apart from the groups in which they take place? How can we have—parallel to the way Kuhn acknowledges there can be "good reasons" for choosing one scientific theory over another—"good reasons" for changing or even rejecting an ethical system?

MacIntyre has recently been attempting to answer such questions.[15] In the Postscript to his widely acclaimed book *After Virtue*, he argues that one ethical system or tradition can be better than another in essentially the same way as one scientific theory can be better than another. In neither case can we hope to find a perfect theory or system, one that can be known to be correct. What we can do is try to find the best one so far. And we can do this, he says, even though there is no foundation independent of any theories or systems, and evaluation must inevitably be done from within one—two points about which he is, if anything, even more adamant in his most recent book, *Whose Justice? Which Rationality?* Rival systems will have common aspects, MacIntyre believes, making it possible at least sometimes for adherents of one to understand and evaluate by their own standards what the adherents of the other are saying. And what they say will include challenges to each other's positions. A given ethical system or tradition may, like a given scientific theory, have "weaknesses, ... inabilities to formulate or solve problems adequately, ... a variety of incoherences"[16] for which a rival one offers cogent explanations. In encountering other traditions, you may thus find good reasons for modifying or deserting your own, in terms of the standards of your own tradition itself.

It seems to us that the first part of this is right: theories can be better than one another in ethics in much the same way as in science. But the process of evaluation would seem to involve more than just theories or traditions themselves. Neither a scientific nor an ethical judgment could be ultimately justifiable—even in a fallible, tentative way—if there were only theories or systems or traditions, and they did not deal with anything beyond themselves alone. Scientific theories are not like this. They deal with our experience, our observations; indeed, they constitute attempts to explain or make sense of these observations. While what we observe is not unaffected by our theories, it is hardly fully determined by them. Had Bodin looked at Venus through a telescope at an appropriate time, he would have seen nearly its full face, and not just the crescent expected on geocentric theory. A scientific theory's strengths and weaknesses and problem-solving abilities can be judged in terms of the explanations that it offers of observations, or that it holds promise of offering.

Observation thus provides a kind of ground for science—not a permanent, absolute foundation, but a possible tentative foothold in what would otherwise be an eternal attempt to lift ourselves by our bootstraps. Any observations can themselves be questioned, but they have to be taken into account—theories cannot simply ignore the observations that appear to go against them. You can question the meaning of observations made through a telescope, but you cannot throw telescopes away once they exist. The better of two conflicting theories is the one which provides, or promises to provide, the better explanation of our experience, and the "best theory so far" is the one that provides or promises to provide the best explanation.

If there is nothing which stands in relation to ethical systems as observation stands to scientific theories, then ethical statements, unlike scientific ones, are not ultimately justifiable. How could we judge the respective cogencies of different ethical traditions, how could we tell whether they are weak or powerful, compelling or shallow, unless they have some sort of aim that relates to something beyond themselves? How could one ethical scheme be better than another unless there is something—like the explanation of observation for scientific theories—which they are both trying to accomplish?

But *isn't* there something ethical systems aim at achieving? Don't they have a point and purpose too? They tell us how to conduct ourselves; isn't this to be towards some end? One of the ideas that we have been arguing for throughout this book—an idea urged by Plato, Aristotle, Buddha, and Confucius, as well as David Hume—is that the reason for being ethical is certain desires we ourselves possess. Perhaps the aim of ethical systems is to tell us how to conduct ourselves so that our behavior will be in line with certain of our desires.

This was, of course, how ethics was understood in the classical Greek tradition. Ethical behavior was behavior in line with those ends that we, as human beings, all possess. But the individual's ends do not necessarily coincide with those of the group, and ethics seems centrally social, seems to concern not our private good but the good of all of us. Suppose, then, that instead of defining ethics in terms of the ends each of us possesses as a human being, we define it in terms of our *common* ends. May the point of ethics be found in our desires for the common good, for ways we all really want the world to be, regardless of our particular positions, experiences, or group memberships? And may this provide the solution to how ethics can be justified? Does the meaning of something's being good ultimately come down to its furthering our shared ends, and of something's being bad, that it stands in their way? May this be the embedded argument that lends such otherwise inexplicable urgency to our moral rhetoric? May such ends be the chords that Gadamerian conversation can hope to strike?

We do not hear much these days about ends that are common to all the varied specimens of humanity. Many currently writing on these matters do not seem to believe there are such ends. MacIntyre, ironically enough (since he champions Aristotle), is one of them: he stresses shared ends, but seems to think they exist only within particular communities. The philosopher Richard Rorty recommends that we see ourselves "as random assemblages of contingent and idiosyncratic needs," [17] and "as having the beliefs and emotions we do, including our (putatively) 'specifically moral' beliefs and emotions, because of some very particular, idiosyncratic things." [18] Some regard human nature itself, no matter how visceral a part of it we contemplate, as a social construction—a product of particular historical circumstances without any claim to generality. [19] Even Barry Schwartz, a psychologist who, like us, wants to undo the prevailing presumption that human beings are necessarily egoistic, argues not that our nature is different from that, but that we don't really have a nature at all—our nature is a block of marble to be sculpted by culture.[20] As Rorty puts it: "There is nothing to people except what has been socialized into them."[21]

Certainly there is enormous variation in what human beings want, depending on happenstances of background and the vagaries of experience, but this does not gainsay some desires possessed by all members of the species. And certainly there are enormous differences in views of our nature in different places and at different times, but this does not render all such views equally fictive; some may be less fictive than others. It would seem hard to deny that we all have desires for personal sustenance, say. We claim it is hard to deny that we all share some desires for common ends as well. All human beings, we submit, would rather live in certain kinds of worlds—have some preferences in common for how life is arranged. Does it seem plausible—especially in view of the sociality of young children and the evolutionary reasons to expect such sociality described in chapter 5—that having there be societies or communities at all is not something we humans really want, whatever our backgrounds?

The very existence of any society would seem to necessitate certain virtues, as MacIntyre himself wrote earlier.[22] There cannot be language without truth-telling. There cannot be roles or functions if carrying them out is not valued. There cannot be agreements or contracts without the virtue of keeping one's word. Here already is a core of characteristics, centering on notions like commitment, faithfulness, trustworthiness, that seem necessary for the furtherance of common ends we share.

There is an East African group called the Ik,[23] who are often cited in attempts to show that ethics cannot be based on anything inherent in human nature. The Ik were a hunting people, whose land and hence way of life were taken from them, and whose ethics then largely disappeared also. What interactions they had were mostly exploitative; they would practice deceit whenever that might gain them anything; they seemed to find cause only for merriment in the suffering of others; they stole from everyone, including stealing food from their parents who were dying of starvation; and they turned those dying parents away when they came pleading to be let in their homes. Colin Turnbull, the anthropologist who made all this known, claims that the Ik demonstrate "that man is not the social animal he has always thought himself to be,"[24] and "that our much vaunted human values are not inherent in humanity at all."[25] Turnbull fears, as we do also, that our own culture is moving in the direction of that of the Ik, and urges that we recognize our Ik-like forms of conduct and mend our ways before it is too late.

This is an effort in which we would like to share. But it seems to us that the lesson of the Ik is not that ethics has no foundation in human nature. After the changes that left them exploitative and treacherous, the Ik were hardly a happy people, and those who were old enough to remember the earlier time deeply mourned its passing. An old, blind woman to whose needs Turnbull and a colleague had ministered suddenly began crying. At first Turnbull thought she needed further assistance, but the reason she was crying, she explained, was that they "had reminded her that there had been a time when people had helped each other, when people had been kind and good." [26]

If human nature is so malleable, if we could equally well develop one way as another, why would there be such grief—or are we to see it as mere nostalgia? Indeed, if social life really did not matter for human beings, if we could flourish as well without community and mutual responsibility as with them, why *should* we worry about our losing them? Would not Turnbull just be giving us propaganda for an arbitrary value preference? The lesson of the Ik, it seems to us, is rather that these *can* be lost—and how precious they are. Once again—as Plato, Aristotle, Buddha, and Confucius stressed—while morality is something we ourselves really want, it is not something that we just spontaneously come by and automatically apply as a guide to our action. Without consciousness-raising, cultivation, and effort, it may disappear.

If it is correct that human beings hold certain preferences in common for the kinds of worlds they would rather inhabit, and that the point and purpose of ethics is the furtherance of those common ends, then a way is open for the justification of ethical beliefs. Ethical schemes can be evaluated on the basis of the extent to which they bring us closer to the common ends we share. We have much to learn about these ends. It would be presumptuous to think the answers are already in hand. But our experience of the human world can serve as an always tentative, fallible ground for the development of such knowledge, just as our experience of the physical world can serve as such a ground for the development of physical knowledge. There already seems every reason to believe that a preference for social life, and the implications of that preference, will be prominent among our common ends.

Ethics, then, becomes a matter of the continuing consideration of what best contributes to our shared common ends, as science is a matter of the continuing consideration of what best explains our observations. And we can make mistakes about what people—including ourselves—really want, but we can also come to recognize those mistakes for what they are.

In our opinion, ethical minimalists may be making such a mistake—failing to recognize some of their own desires. They may have become misled about the requirements for their own best flourishing. They too, we think, would rather live in a world in which responsibilities are exercised, in which commitments are fulfilled, in which people look out for and care for one another, and would rather contribute to such a world. The difference between that kind of world and the world of the Ik is not just an arbitrary matter.

This is not to say that one is ever justified in taking for granted what another's real wants are and insisting that they behave accordingly. Claiming to know what is best for another is an old authoritarian ploy. Autonomy is to be preserved and all you have a right to insist on from someone else is non-infringement. But perhaps we could be a little less ready to accept therapeutically whatever anyone says as "right for them," and a little more willing to undertake the risks of Gadamerian conversation.

Minimalists have certain views about the requirements for their own thriving, and this book is an attempt to convince them otherwise. It asks whether they themselves would not rather be like those we interviewed who go beyond a minimal ethic, at least if others were like that too. And it inquires whether minimalists may not have been blinded to some of their own desires along these lines by the assumptive frameworks for thinking about ethics to which they as contemporary Westerners are heirs. In so doing, the book tries, as it were, to engage them in Gadamerian conversation—albeit necessarily of a one-sided kind, given the nature of book writing. The other party to the conversation has to be heard from.

The hope of such an effort is to make a start toward unchaining ourselves from the perpetual see-saw between liberal license and authoritarian reaction. We have argued that staying bound to this see-saw is as unnecessary as it is tragic. Liberals are wrong about what autonomy requires. Authoritarians are wrong about what morality requires. The untenability of the choice created by these errors erodes our civility as a society.

7

Some Thoughts for Feminists, Communitarians, and Moral Educators

In the modern and postmodern age, there has been greater awareness than ever before of the ubiquity of human beings' oppression of one another and stronger urges than ever before to fight for freedom and justice. The autonomy virus in its many forms has proved to be catching indeed and to defy regional quarantine. Imperialism, while it has hardly disappeared, is increasingly subject to challenge. Left-wing as well as right-wing varieties of coercion and control can no longer be practiced with impunity or with confidence that a day of reckoning will never come. Days of reckoning have been coming, they can come, and wielders of power show at the least a refreshing nervousness about their grounds to legitimacy. In more tolerant settings, further levels of liberty are claimed against encroachment by the state; and attempts are under way to secure the rights of the poor, minorities, women, the handicapped, and individuals who are gay. Combatting domination, being autonomous and respecting the autonomy of others—these are crucial concerns to many, and we would count ourselves among them.

This book has been directed at those who, in the name of freedom and autonomy, seek liberation from whatever may restrain personal development, self-expression, pursuit of personal ends—often losing sight in the process of the common good and the meaningfulness of taking on roles aimed at serving it. This book also has been directed at those who find themselves on the defensive against accusations of illiberality for sensing something wrong with the personal license that liberalism seems to grant. It endorses practices that can look naive to the sophisticated and overly earnest to the cynical. It argues for viewing work and effort not only as a means of achieving status, prestige, self-enhancement, self-fulfillment, besides making a living, but—even when in conflict with what may be personally most actualizing—as an opportunity for contribution. It argues for having roles and taking them seriously as reminders and definers of ideals of conduct, for taking promises and commitments seriously as inherently meaningful to make and keep, for honoring the trust that is placed in each individual by others and by society. It argues for weighing the implications of what one does in life against the daunting standard of trying to "make the world a better place," despite the difficulty of knowing what will do that. And it argues for teaching these things to the young.

"Traditional values," then? Are we simply adding our voices to the conservative cry for a return to the old-fashioned virtues? Yes—and no. Some of those virtues—like the serious consideration of what trust and roles require of us—seem central enough to a viable future that leaving them adrift as matters of taste is cultural suicide. But they are not to be based on overt or covert applications of force, either. They are not to be obtained at the cost of justice and freedom—these "liberal" values are essential. To be moral, we believe, you must *at least* not infringe on anyone's rights, even though this alone is far from enough for morality.

Justice and autonomy are necessary, but not sufficient. What we are trying to combat is the frequently encountered situation where attention to these has the effect of pushing people away from one another—of severing bonds and connections, whether in a family or a society—and reinforcing self-focus and pursuit of the personal. It seems to us crucial that those traditional virtues that knit people into communities and promote their carrying out functions for one another be retained—but not at the expense of the liberal virtues of autonomy, respect, and justice. Our central effort has been to show that, contrary to what is repeatedly taken for granted, these are not incompatible, but can and need to be integrated. In this chapter we will say a little about what this means in relation to several current social issues: feminism, community, and moral education.

Feminism

Take feminism first. It can hardly be doubted that despite liberalism, despite a great many efforts on the part of a great many people, despite recent changes in laws and institutions, women in our society (and most others as well) are hindered in various ways from attaining full measures of freedom and autonomy. Indeed, we would like to see more real autonomy for men as well as women, but women lag far behind. Considerable distance must be bridged before women will be as free as men are now to choose what to do with themselves, what to make of their lives. There is a similarly long way to go before women will be listened to and respected as much as men are now—by men and by themselves. These points do not imply, however, as some feminists have thought, that women are to become like the stereotype of men: separate, aggressive, power-grasping, oriented wholly to their own development and achievement. Nor do these points imply that women must give up their connectedness and warmth and nurturance, that compassion is a "trap," [1] or that motherhood is "a condition of terminal psychological and social decay, total self-abnegation and physical deterioration." [2]

The economist Sylvia Ann Hewlett [3] has made a compelling case that feminists' doubts about motherhood and families have in fact, at least until recently, led them to ignore the strongest interests of most women. Child care and anything else related to children have tended to receive a low priority on the political agendas of feminist groups; matters like part-time and flexible-time employment arrangements have usually not been considered at all. Legislation for maternity leave has even been opposed, as conflicting with equal treatment. When a 1979 California law which provided four months of unpaid leave for medical disability resulting from pregnancy or childbirth was challenged by the California Chamber of Commerce and a group of employers, the National Organization for Women (NOW) filed a brief in their support. [4]

Ignoring children and what is involved in bearing them and caring for them in pursuit of a goal of unisex treatment seems in effect like collusion with conservatives in their ignoring of the fact that most women are working. Downplaying motherhood cannot, in our opinion, help serve women's interests. In 1980, ninety percent of all American women between the ages of forty and forty-four had children. [5] It is hard at a time of relative sophistication and expertise about contraception to see all of this as a male conspiracy, rather than as what at least many of these women—really—want.

In the last dozen years or so, many feminists have come to take a much more positive stance towards motherhood and towards "feminine" qualities like nurturance, warmth, and compassion. This is associated most strongly with the work of Carol Gilligan, who contends that on matters regarding values, self, and relationships, we need to listen to "a different voice" than the one we usually hear. [6] The dominant voice, one that is heard typically from men and not women, speaks of justice and autonomy. Implicit here is "a view of the individual as separate and of relationships as either hierarchical or contractual." [7] The voice to which we need to listen, the unheard voice of women, represents the values of care and connection. Implicit in this voice is "a view of the self and other as interdependent and of relationships as networks sustained by care-giving and response." [8]

A man illustrating the first perspective says, when asked what morality means to him: "I think it is recognizing the right of the individual, the rights of other individuals, not interfering with those rights. Act as fairly as you would have them treat you." [9] A woman illustrating the second says, in response to the same question: "a person's life is enriched by cooperating with other people and striving to live in harmony with everybody else, and to that end, there are right and wrong, there are things which promote that end and that move away from it." [10]

Gilligan regards these two orientations—the dominant, more "masculine" one, and the more "feminine" one to which she is calling attention—as unitary and different alternatives, each necessary as a kind of correction to the other, but not capable of being put together or really integrated. [11] She likes to compare them to the shifting figure-ground perceptions available in ambiguous visual patterns, where a given figural organization makes the other disappear, as when one can see *either* a vase *or* two faces but never both at once. [12] At a recent conference of psychologists and philosophers, [13] Gilligan repeatedly rejected any suggestion that her perspectives could be assimilated to one another or be in any way synthesized. Since for Gilligan they are analogous to alternative figural organizations, they cannot be reconciled: more time seeing the one has to mean less time seeing the other.

We believe, of course, that Gilligan has performed an important service in calling attention to the moral significance of care and connection. But once again communion and altruism are being pitted against autonomy. If these values must forever conflict, then the message would seem to be at best an ambivalent one. Care seems denigrated by understanding it as opposed to individuation. If I can only care with some sacrifice of freedom and justice, how much will I want to care?

Why is Gilligan so convinced that the two voices must remain separate—that they cannot be unified? She apparently believes that they embody a number of conflicting conceptions: reason versus feeling, impartial general rules versus response to the particular, separation versus connection. On closer inspection, however, none of these oppositions in themselves seem to be irreconcilable. Take reason and feeling first. It is of course very widely assumed that these are antithetical, but we have already seen that this view seems incorrect. We have discussed in chapter 4 how reason can in fact affect action only in combination with feeling—with something you care about. As Hume pointed out, reason per se supplies no ends; there must ultimately be "something desirable on its own account" that motivates our action—some end we seek to further. To be moved to purposive action, we have to care about or want some result. Reason may sometimes deteriorate in the heat of strong feeling, but it must function together with feeling if it is to have any impact at all on what we do. Even being just is not something we must do if we are to be rational, but something we must do if we care enough about justice.

Consider next the antinomy of impartial general rules versus response to the particular. It is true that the impartiality of justice can conflict with the partiality of care. Care pulls me more toward feeding my own child; justice pulls me more toward children who are starving in Africa. But these are both valid pulls and neither vitiates the other. What I have to do is arrive at some resolution taking both into account—no doubt putting my own child's hunger before that of the African children, but perhaps putting their hunger before expensive luxuries for my child.[14] Few would consider me unjust if this becomes my order of priorities. Justice does not require that we pay no greater attention to those closest to us than to anyone else. The impartiality it demands is limited: there are certain rights we must grant to all, avoiding nepotistic favors that would compromise those rights, but we are not obligated to treat everyone equally in all respects.

Gilligan also sometimes speaks of the significance of contextual detail for feminine morality, as opposed to the abstract generality of justice. We must admit to qualms about Gilligan's breathing new life here into the old stereotype that makes women concrete thinkers suitable for comparison with schizophrenics and the brain-damaged. But though it is probably true that women tend to pay more attention to context than men do, context does not seem irrelevant to justice any more than it does to care. The defining of extenuating circumstances has a large part to play in legal construals of guilt and innocence.

What seems most central to Gilligan's conviction that the perspectives are irreconcilable is the opposition between separation and connection. It is quite true that conceiving of others as adversaries conflicts with seeing them as allies. If I am concerned about your granting me my rights and autonomy, I am not thinking about us as tied together by mutual response and care. This is in itself an important point, one that has perhaps been insufficiently taken into account by those feminists who have a constant, overriding concern with equality, and by some marriage counselors. Insisting on extracting our rights from one another is not always the best immediate response to injury or potential injury—sometimes others will themselves want to act differently when they know their actions are harmful. Nonetheless, sometimes we must insist on our rights—and when we do, this does make positive connection difficult, at least temporarily. Insofar as I focus on obtaining justice from you, this is, admittedly, hard to reconcile with a focus on caring for you.

However, *being* just is not at all incompatible with care and connection. On the contrary, my care for you is likely to make me want to avoid oppressing or dominating you, or allowing anyone else to do so. Precisely because I care about you, it will matter to me that you be treated fairly. (And perhaps also that you be fair yourself.)

Is being *autonomous* incompatible with connection and care? Gilligan believes that it is. Philosophers, in responding to her, have formulated particular senses of autonomy that do not seem to exclude care, such as freedom from neurotic impulse, or taking responsibility.[15] But it seems to us that the reason Gilligan views autonomy as incompatible with care in the first place is that, once again, she is confounding autonomy with a focus on the self. We have been arguing throughout this book that the range of my real wants extends beyond the circle of personal benefit. To think for myself and decide for myself does not, then, mean that I will do only what is good for myself. Considering the good of others does not have to derive only from external pressures or forces. Indeed, we have found the likelihood high that there are innate grounds for concern for others in all of us. Care and connectedness are thus part of what we can autonomously want and choose.

An illustration of autonomous care is provided by one of the women quoted in Gilligan's own work, though unremarked by Gilligan. This woman, in her late twenties, says, "I think I have a real drive, a real maternal drive, to take care of someone—to take care of my mother, to take care of children, to take care of other people's children, to take care of my own children, to take care of the world. When I am dealing with moral issues, I am sort of saying to myself constantly, 'Are you taking care of all the things that you think are important?'" [16]

Autonomy doesn't have to separate us from each other. Actually, I can be a much more effective ally of yours if I retain my autonomy. If I am afraid to do anything that displeases you, I may, for example (as with many a submissive wife) avoid telling you something you would not like to hear but that it would be better for you to learn about. [17] Aristotle well understood this point when he considered the nature of friendship: a true friend of yours is not a sycophant, but someone willing to risk your anger for the sake of what you ought to know. Quite generally, if I do not think for myself, but—whether in the name of tolerance or out of fear— uncritically accept others' views and opinions, I will not be able to enter into Gadamerian conversation with them, helping each of us to a better grasp of what we may see wrongly. Abdication of independent judgment is hardly what is called for by care.

The principles of justice and autonomy do not, then, seem irreconcilable to care and connection. They are not, as Gilligan would have it, alternate ways of seeing. Justice and autonomy, we believe, constitute not a full morality but rather a kind of starting point: necessary but not sufficient. Morality requires as a first step that we refrain from treading on others' rights, but justice only, without care, hardly seems satisfactory in any instance for anybody. Both are always crucial—and there is no reason that they cannot be integrated. It is only when people *fail* to respect one anothers' rights that dissonance arises between the perspectives of justice and care. A morality of justice and autonomy is not a real competitor, then, against a morality of concern and care. We need them both—in the same heads at the same time. It is not unrealistic, with discipline and cultivation, to expect to find them there.

Community

And we need them both, not only for small social units like families or groups of friends, but for large ones including nation-states. This has serious implications for politics. It means that the aim of the political process is not—as in the widely prevailing view—simply the furtherance of the (enlightened) self-interests of those concerned. Social contract theories, from Hobbes and Locke to Freud to Robert Nozick, have typically based the authority of government and the obligation of the citizen on those individual interests. A political union is seen essentially as a kind of arrangement in which each member contracts to renounce certain possibilities, such as attacking one's neighbor, in order that others shall do likewise, such as refrain from attacking in return. It is a bleak picture of mutual standoff. As the political philosopher Benjamin Barber has put this, "politics is prudence in the service of *homo economicus*—the solitary seeker of material happiness and bodily security." [18] Political life, as described by another social thinker, William Sullivan, becomes a matter of "contracting individuals indifferent to each other, sharing nothing except a nervous regard for certain rules of procedure." [19]

If, as we have been arguing, human beings are far from appropriately portrayed as solitary and indifferent to one another—if our very nature includes proclivities to connect, to care, to contribute—then political life should, rather, constitute a mutual association for the common good, in which personal goals are not all that matters. It should become a considering together and a joint attempt to further that good. My task becomes envisioning what will be best for a larger polity, not how to use others for my own purposes. For example, let me envision how better to provide for our country's children, a greater percentage of whom live in poverty than any other age group, [20] and for whom the quality of care is often abysmal. Large numbers of day care arrangements are unsafe, unhealthy, and hardly nurturing of constructive development. Two to seven million school-age children are left without any care at all after school is out. [21] Meanwhile in many states legislation that has been in place for years requires the father's absence as a condition of eligibility for aid. Or let me envision how to stop the devastation of our planet, including the rapid accumulation of radioactive wastes that lose only half their strength in 24,000 years, and for which no known method of safe disposal exists. [22] Are we to say, with an economist at the

University of London: "Suppose that...human life did come to an end. So what?" [23] Or would we rather be like the person of the future in Marge Piercy's novel, *Woman on the Edge of Time*, who, when asked whether nothing gets thrown away in her time, asks in turn, "Thrown away where? The world is round." [24]

We are, of course, fortunately far from alone in touting the common good. Politics is not always thought of in terms of negotiations among individuals or groups with varying special interests. Not everyone believes that social life is a matter of doing what will further your own particular ends, or what you have contracted towards facilitating their attainment—that otherwise you are letting yourself be imposed upon, dominated, oppressed. In the first period of our country's history, the central idea of virtue was the subordination of private wants to the public interest. [25] And this is an idea that continues. The political philosopher and activist Marcus Raskin, for example, recently wrote a book entitled, *The Common Good: Its Politics, Policies, and Philosophy*. [26] The book by Robert Bellah and his associates, *Habits of the Heart*, [27] and the earlier work by one of that book's co-authors, William Sullivan's *Reconstructing Public Philosophy*, [28] are devoted to showing the limitations of our typical individualism and attempting to revive the community concern of the tradition of civic republicanism. Michael Sandel, another political philosopher, has written one book [29] and edited another [30] criticizing the individualistic aspects of liberalism and propounding a communitarian view instead.

While communitarians are urging more attention to the common good, however, they often seem to vitiate the very idea of individual autonomy in the process. It is not that they fail to recognize the cruciality of preventing people with power from claiming special knowledge of that good and imposing their values on those who are weaker. They tend to stress democracy, as participatory a form of it as possible, and to argue that it is precisely to the extent that we lack a public life and a sense of common involvement that we are vulnerable to authoritarianism. [31] But they typically tie their emphasis on community goals to a social determinism in which our aims and purposes are seen as a function of our societies and our socialization. We are who we are and we want what we want because of the particular communities we live in. [32] Communitarian goals are thus conceived as inevitably internalized from the groups in which we develop, the groups whose practices we happen to share.

If this is their basis, communitarian goals hardly qualify as autonomous ones. We do not necessarily want to accept those aims and values which we have acquired through socialization. I may have been raised with the notion of white supremacy, but want to free myself of racism. I may have grown up in an ethnic subculture that imbued its members with strong competitive strivings, but find this response deeply troubling. I may have experienced the comradeship of participation in the Hitler Youth and gone on to become a Nazi, and now be nauseated by my past. Are any possible changes just a question of equally arbitrary "resocialization"—new groups replacing old?

The danger of grounding values on existing community traditions is well illustrated by the following (rather astounding) statement by a Senior Research Fellow at Stanford University in an article in the 1986 *World Book Encyclopedia:*

> "Suppose a political scientist wishes to determine scientifically whether a particular community should have an authoritarian or a representative form of political organization and control. The scholar must first learn the importance the community attaches to such values as the right of the individual to differ with authority, or to have a voice in policy and laws. Then the principles that govern its political action can be formulated." [33]

What should be follows from whatever the tradition is. So much for the significance of democracy.

Communitarians are not likely to have any difficulty in getting minimalists to agree with them that communitarian ends are the consequence of socialization, but minimalists will insist—rightly, we believe—that this does not provide any valid ground for embracing these ends. Accepting them by virtue of one's socialization would be tantamount to submitting to indoctrination. Calling upon community tradition will thus not be an effective way of arguing for attention to the common good. It smacks of the "blood and soil" appeals to group solidarity that liberals rightly fear. Does a communitarian then have no answer to a minimalist?

When we hear people say, as now happens all too frequently, that ethics asks no more of them than pursuit of their personal goals and allowing others to do likewise, is there no valid argument against them? Is there nothing to offer by way of rebuttal that might change their minds? Perhaps a sneak attack is the answer: perhaps they will agree to some part of a tradition that allows the desirability of communitarian ends to be derived from it. But this desirability seems basic enough that if someone rejected communitarian claims, it is hard to imagine they would still adhere to other aspects of a tradition from which the value of community could suddenly and miraculously be derived. Their whole point would be freedom from the shackles of community intrusiveness that restrict our choices in the hallowed name of heritage. And what if—as happened with the East African Ik and seems dangerously close to happening in our own case also—attention to the common good itself wanes from a tradition? Is there no rational basis for seeking to resuscitate it? Has a communitarian no legitimate defense against the charge of simply preferring the ways of yesteryear over those of today?

The usual communitarian view is right, we think, that the source of communitarian ends lies within ourselves. But that source need not only be our tradition, or something we have internalized from our group. The ultimate ground for pursuit of interests beyond the personal lies rather, we believe, in human nature.

There seems to be a strong case, as we argued in chapter 5, that there is good in our genes—not good alone, but some good. In terms of everything now known, it appears extremely likely that our species has evolved a tendency toward concern for others. Very young infants seem disturbed when those about them show signs of distress; very small children make efforts to help and comfort others. The ages in question make the learning of personally adverse implications an unlikely explanation for such reactions. The problem of free riders has recently led many to doubt the natural selection of tendencies to helpfulness other than in the case of kin. Our earlier discussion showed, however, that this now appears to have been a mistaken conclusion. Proximity and familiarity can serve as proxies for kin, leading "near" to be treated as "dear" even without genes in common. Also, once individuals can recognize one another, there is the possibility of reciprocal help-giving, which itself makes likely the evolutionary selection of a tendency to be helpful on first encounters and to continue so long as the other does likewise. Further, as evolutionary biologist David Sloan Wilson has shown, when individuals mostly interact within smaller groups while young but disperse at maturity, the beneficial effects of helpfulness within a group should lead to its selection, quite apart from reciprocation, despite free riders.

It does not seem to be just because we are socialized into given traditions that we would rather live in a manner such that the needs of other people's children are met and the planet given a relatively uncontaminated future. If someone asks why they should consider more than just their personal goals, with others free to do the same, here is a possible answer: "I think in fact there is more that matters to you, and not just from having been inducted into the ways of a given society but as part of the kind of animal you are." Communitarians may have a better basis for their hopes than they have understood—and a needed basis if they are to escape relativism.

Moral Education

It is their apparent vulnerability to the accusation of historical contingency—of stemming merely from a particular tradition—that undercuts communitarian arguments. The real basis, even if kept under wraps, is then a tradition's arbitrary authority—the irrational residues of socialization—with no claim to greater warrant than the alternative tradition of another group. Moral education that goes beyond minimalism then can only be indoctrination: parents and teachers cementing the claims of their values by dint of superior power. Whatever the rhetoric of justification, the child is to be bent in a particular direction because of membership in a particular group, whether defined in religious, national, ethnic, historical, or any other terms. The agenda becomes inculcating a particular tradition's "bag of virtues," to use the moral educator Lawrence Kohlberg's derisory phrase. And this curtailment of autonomy in the name of a particular tradition's notion of the greater good is what liberals cannot accept.

In the face of moral disarray, however, traditionalist calls to character education take on renewed urgency and gain new recruits. Our own society bears current witness to this effect in ways too obvious and numerous to dwell upon. Morals *must* be inculcated, it is asserted; behavior that does not conform to the norm must be punished, physically if necessary; religion or at least strong authority must be brought back into the schools. Autonomy is ceded to virtues which receive hard or soft sells in attempts to influence how young people will think and act. These authoritarian reactions to what is perceived as "permissiveness" seem inevitable when attempts by liberal educators to teach morality founder on what they take to be autonomy's requirements. The

Thoughts for Feminists, Communitarians, & Moral Educators   129

logic of their position, however much they may protest, corners them into supporting minimalism—precisely the problem that fuels their opposition. Consider how this works.

Two recent waves of renewed interest in moral education have been premised on the autonomy focus of liberalism: values clarification and Kohlberg's moral developmentalism. In the case of values clarification, the support for a minimalist ethic stems rather directly from Rogerian therapy. Values clarification represents an extension to the schools of Carl Rogers's therapeutic injunction to get in touch with one's own feelings and make choices on the basis of them. Teachers, like therapists, are to function as non-judgmental facilitators of this process, avoiding moralizing or criticism, providing support and acceptance of each individual's personal quest. Outside limits will have to be set, of course—those of not permitting choices that clearly harm others. But the rest is viewed as a personal matter; the important thing is to learn how to make one's life choices in as uncoerced a way as possible.

Prescriptions and restraints serve on this view only to cloud our awareness of spontaneous likes and dislikes. As one of the founders of the values clarification movement puts it, life is viewed as a "lovely banquet" to be negotiated. [34] The point, then, is to find out what dishes please you and to eat them. You are entitled to your preferences, and these are to be discovered, not cultivated or improved.

Equally concerned to avoid indoctrination has been Lawrence Kohlberg, who for some thirty years until his recent death did a great deal to rehabilitate morality's study within a liberal psychology that had been made uncomfortable by the idea of morality as authoritarian imposition. He replaced that idea with a more congenial Deweyite emphasis on children's thinking for themselves. But instead of positing personal autonomy as the authenticating prerequisite for all choices, in the manner of the values clarifiers, Kohlberg set autonomy as the endpoint of a process of moral development. He avoids relativism as well as indoctrination by regarding later stages in this development as objectively higher and better.

Moral thinking starts, in Kohlberg's developmental scheme, at a "preconventional" level at which the child takes a strictly individualistic perspective. What is right is essentially what is to one's own benefit. Rules and expectations are followed on the basis of externally imposed rewards and punishments. Then—hopefully— children proceed to a "conventional" level, at which they no longer take an individualistic but now a social point of view. The right or the good now depends not just on what benefits you but also on what benefits other individuals or the group as a whole. Here we have what is often regarded as the essence of morality. But at this level, one is not autonomous. Socialization has taken place: one has internalized (in the manner of social learning theory, for which, however, this is the final accomplishment) the rules and expectations of others, so that sanctions are now self-administered.

To become autonomous one must advance to a third level, a "postconventional" one, which "returns us to the standpoint of the individual rather than taking the point of view of 'us members of society.'" [35] The self no longer functions here as a precipitate of social identifications. Adopting a "prior-to-society" perspective, it proceeds as a free agent, treating others as equally free agents. Morality is now a matter of following universal principles of justice, respect, and equal rights. At the highest stage, everybody ends up with as much personal freedom as possible commensurate with granting the same to everyone else—in Kohlberg's words, "the maximum liberty compatible with the like liberty of others." [36]

Movement from lower to higher stages is thought to make possible successively more adequate solutions of moral problems. At the conventional level you have no way to support the conventions of your group against someone who challenges these conventions, and no way to evaluate suggested changes. [37] At the postconventional level you are able to call upon universal principles of freedom and equality with which Kohlberg thought any rational person must agree. The progression of stages provides "a way out from the Scylla of indoctrination and the Charybdis of 'laid-back' relativism or values clarification." [38] It is a natural process which can be facilitated by democratic discussion of ethical quandaries; this will lead you to stage progression without others acting as authorities telling you what is right or good. Rather, you will see for yourself when the proposals of others make for better solutions than you were able to provide—moral education without indoctrination and without relativism.

What Kohlberg's developmental scheme suggests, however, is an inevitable march toward minimalism as the moral ideal. At the postconventional level, I must grant equal rights to all, but others have no claim on me apart from justice. By contrast, it is at the conventional level of moral development that sociality reigns—a dominion that is to give way to autonomy when and if the postconventional level is reached. Sociality in this framework has an inferior status; it implies dependence and conformity. Society, whether in the form of one other person or many, is inherently oppressive, imposing itself in a manner acceptable to social learning theorists or to Freud, and indeed viewed as necessary by them for the common good, but which Kohlberg wants his thinkers to surmount. The individual has to become free of direct (preconventional level) and indirect (conventional level) forms of imposition. We are to arrive at the position (postconventional level) of respecting one another's autonomy to do as we please without infringing on each other.

Here are moral reasoning responses that qualify as postconventional according to Kohlberg's scoring system. The examples come from the Kohlberg group's own scoring. Asked what morality or morally right means to him, a twenty-four-year-old man replies: "Recognizing the rights of other individuals, first to life and then to do as he pleases as long as it doesn't interfere with somebody else's rights." [39] A twenty-five-year-old man talks of morality as meaning "basically to preserve the human being's right to existence.... Secondly, the human being's rights to do as he pleases, again without interfering with somebody else's rights." [40] As these responses indicate, minimalists are categorized as postconventional thinkers. In Kohlberg's system, minimalism is developmentally superior.

Kohlberg cared about community, and deeply so. His life testified to no less. He wanted others to care about it as well. In recent years he and his students attempted to create "just communities"—what they viewed as ideal miniature societies—in a number of different schools. These were to be as democratic as possible, but Kohlberg now softened his previous insistence on nonindoctrination. [41] The goal no longer was furthering development to the highest possible stage. Instead it now was solid attainment of the conventional level "commitment of being a good member of a community or a good citizen." [42] Such commitment had become more important than moving towards postconventionality. [43] Community, it seems, was of greater significance to Kohlberg than his developmental scheme permitted.

He did make various modifications in that scheme over the years, some of which granted a little more weight to the values of community and social concern. There were repeated revisions in the detailed conceptualization of the stages and in their scoring systems. [44] The possibility even was broached of an additional, perhaps religious, stage "based on an ethic that goes beyond, and is higher than, an ethic of justice." [45] But the discrepancy between Kohlberg's theory and the significance—to him as to us—of the social has not been satisfactorily resolved. This discrepancy in fact would seem fated to remain, whatever additions or alterations are made, since underlying Kohlberg's entire scheme is the conception that as you develop, you become more autonomous, and as you become more autonomous, you become, of necessity, more detached and more purely rational.

Nor is the answer the one provided by Carol Gilligan, who accepts Kohlberg's interpretation of what autonomy implies, and calls for equal time for an irreconcilable feminine morality of care. The problem dissolves if autonomy need not mean detachment. For then the looking inward of the values clarifiers or the detached attitude of Kohlberg's postconventional level are no longer the only ways to attain freedom. If we are correct in claiming that our biology itself gives us wishes to join together with others and to further their purposes, autonomy is not incompatible with community and care.

The implication of this point for moral education is straightforward. It means there is no reason that encouragement of social concern and community must be indoctrinative or limiting of freedom. Autonomy and respect are indeed crucial. No one is to insist on the correctness of their sense of the good and on others' conformity to it. But we can, with conversation in the Gadamerian mode, help each other to locate resonances within ourselves that support ends outside of us, ends that are not self-referential but that we own nonetheless. We can look for and call attention to exemplars—heroic models, if you will—in narrative as well as in reality, that expose one another to ways and styles of functioning that make sense in terms of our own wants, raising our degree of awareness concerning possibilities we ourselves seek that were not sufficiently envisaged or understood before. And we can ourselves live in ways that reflect larger devotions rather than treating them as forms of masochism.

The confusion of autonomy with self-focus has cast a long shadow. It has led many to believe that substantial ethics can only be maintained at the cost of subjugation, turning some into minimalists and others into authoritarians. It has stopped many from believing they have any right to offer their ethical outlooks to others, even the young. This conviction that autonomy and self-focus must rise or fall together is, we have argued, a mistaken notion born of the externalization of ethics—an externalization that came with the development of Judeo-Christian religious thinking and remained even for those who stopped believing. Evidence from observing infants and children, from biology, and from phenomenology, counters the confusion. It supports the immanence in our species of concerns for our fellows, providing a basis within us for considerations beyond us. Yet there is no reason to expect these concerns will automatically receive the attention we ourselves want for them. That takes effort and cultivation. Perhaps it is time we emerge from the confusion's shadow and recognize that minimalism and authority are not our only choices.

NOTES

Chapter 1

1. Isaiah Berlin, Introduction, in Isaiah Berlin, *Four Essays on Liberty* (Oxford: Oxford University Press, 1969), p. lvi.

2. Berlin, "Two Concepts of Liberty," in Berlin, *Four Essays on Liberty*, p. 153.

3. Quoted from an interview in James S. Fishkin, *Beyond Subjective Morality: Ethical Reasoning and Political Philosophy* (New Haven, Conn.: Yale University Press, 1984), p. 72.

4. James T. Laney, "The Education of the Heart," *Harvard Magazine*, 88, no. 1 (Sept.-Oct. 1985), p. 24.

5. James Atlas, "A Postwar Classic: Reconsideration—Philip Roth's 'Letting Go,'" *The New Republic*, June 2, 1982, p. 28.

6. C. Randall Powell, *Career Planning Today* (Dubuque, Iowa: Kendall/Hunt Publishing Co., 1981), p. 23. The listing of values is on p. 24.

7. See Michael A. Wallach and Lise Wallach, *Psychology's Sanction for Selfishness: The Error of Egoism in Theory and Therapy* (New York: W. H. Freeman and Co., 1983).

8. Darrell Smith, "Trends in Counseling and Psychotherapy," *American Psychologist*, 37 (1982), 808.

9. Carl R. Rogers, *Becoming Partners: Marriage and Its Alternatives* (New York: Dell, 1972), p. 10.

10. Edwin Kahn, "Heinz Kohut and Carl Rogers: A Timely Comparison," *American Psychologist*, 40 (1985), 900.

11. See Stuart T. Hauser, "Loevinger's Model and Measure of Ego Development: A Critical Review," *Psychological Bulletin*, 83 (1976), 928–955.

12. Donald N. McCloskey, "The Literary Character of Economics," *Daedalus*, 113, no. 3 (Summer 1984), 114.

13. McCloskey, "The Literary Character of Economics," p. 103.

14. Amitai Etzioni, "The Case for a Multiple-Utility Conception," *Economics and Philosophy*, 2 (1986), 159–183.

15. Peter Berger, "On the Obsolescence of the Concept of Honor," in Stanley Hauerwas and Alasdair MacIntyre, eds., *Revisions: Changing Perspectives in Moral Philosophy* (Notre Dame, Indiana: University of Notre Dame Press, 1983), p. 177.

16. Richard Sennett, *The Fall of Public Man* (New York: Alfred A. Knopf, 1977), p. 219.

17. Kitty Cunningham with Michael Ballard, *Conversations with a Dancer* (New York: St. Martin's Press, 1980), p. 49.

18. Ada Louise Huxtable, "After Modern Architecture," *The New York Review of Books*, Dec. 8, 1983, p. 34.

19. Quoted from an interview in Robert N. Bellah, Richard Madsen, William M. Sullivan, Ann Swidler, and Steven M. Tipton, *Habits of the Heart: Individualism and Commitment in American Life* (Berkeley, Calif.: University of California Press, 1985), pp. 70–71.

20. Bellah, Madsen, Sullivan, Swidler, and Tipton, *Habits of the Heart*, p. 247.

21. Stanley Hauerwas, "On Keeping Theological Ethics Theological," in Hauerwas and MacIntyre, eds., *Revisions*, p. 35.

22. Allan Bloom, *The Closing of the American Mind* (New York: Simon and Schuster, 1987), p. 337.

23. Jerome Kagan, "The Moral Function of the School," *Daedalus*, 110, no. 3 (Summer 1981), 163.

24. Janet T. Spence, "Achievement American Style: The Rewards and Costs of Individualism." *American Psychologist*, 40 (1985), 1293.

25. John C. Gibbs and Steven V. Schnell, "Moral Development 'versus' Socialization: A Critique," *American Psychologist*, 40 (1985), 1071–1080.

26. Diana Baumrind, "Sex Differences in Moral Reasoning: Response to Walker's (1984) Conclusion That There Are None," *Child Development*, 57 (1986), 519.

27. Carol Gilligan, *In a Different Voice: Psychological Theory and Women's Development* (Cambridge, Mass.: Harvard University Press,

1982), p. 172. See also Carol Gilligan, "Remapping the Moral Domain: New Images of the Self in Relationship," in Thomas C. Heller, Morton Sosna, and David E. Wellbery, eds. *Reconstructing Individualism: Autonomy, Individuality, and the Self in Western Thought* (Stanford, Calif.: Stanford University Press, 1986).

28. Kagan, "The Moral Function of the School," p. 163.

29. Kagan, "The Moral Function of the School," p. 163.

30. William J. Froming, Leticia Allen, and Richard Jensen, "Altruism, Role-Taking, and Self-Awareness: The Acquisition of Norms Governing Altruistic Behavior," *Child Development*, 56 (1985), 1223.

31. Mitch Albom, "Lying to Get Even," *Columbia: The Magazine of Columbia University*, 8, no. 4 (Jan. 1983), 15.

32. Walker Percy, *The Last Gentleman* (New York: Farrar, Straus, and Giroux, 1966).

33. Percy, *The Last Gentleman*, p. 202.

Chapter 3

1. Moses I. Finley, *The World of Odysseus*, 2d ed. (London: Chatto and Windus, 1977), p. 28.

2. A.W.H. Adkins, *Moral Values and Political Behavior in Ancient Greece: From Homer to the End of the Fifth Century* (New York: W. W. Norton and Co., 1972), p. 28.

3. Adkins, *Moral Values and Political Behavior in Ancient Greece*, p. 29. See also his discussion on p. 30.

4. Adkins, *Moral Values and Political Behavior in Ancient Greece*, p. 42.

5. Adkins, *Moral Values and Political Behavior in Ancient Greece*, p. 42.

6. Adkins, *Moral Values and Political Behavior in Ancient Greece*, p. 116. Classicists differ on just what was intended by Orestes's speech, and on whether it is correctly attributed to Euripides. See, for example, Simon Goldhill, "Rhetoric and Relevance: Interpolation at Euripides *Electra* 367–400," *Greek, Roman, and Byzantine Studies*, 27 (1986), 157–171.

7. Adkins, *Moral Values and Political Behavior in Ancient Greece*, p. 117.

8. Plato, Gorgias, 492a, b, c, in W.R.M. Lamb, tr., *Plato: With an English Translation*, vol. 5 (London: William Heinemann, 1925), p. 413.

9. Plato, Gorgias, 508b, p. 471.

10. Plato, Protagoras, 358d, in W.R.M. Lamb, tr., *Plato: With an English Translation*. vol. 4 (London: William Heinemann, 1924), pp. 245-247.

11. Hugh Lloyd-Jones, *The Justice of Zeus* (Berkeley, Calif.: University of California Press, 1971), p. 3.

12. See J. L. Ackrill, *Aristotle on Eudaimonia* (London: Oxford University Press, 1975).

13. Aristotle, *Nicomachean Ethics*, book 7, chap. 2., in Richard McKeon, ed., *Introduction to Aristotle* (New York: Modern Library/Random House, 1947), p. 444.

14. Thomas Marshall, *Aristotle's Theory of Conduct* (London: T. Fisher Unwin, 1906), p. 367.

15. Aristotle, *Nicomachean Ethics*, book 2, chap. 1, in McKeon, ed., *Introduction to Aristotle*, p. 332. Emphasis given in reference.

16. Aristotle, *Nicomachean Ethics*, book 1, chap. 5, in McKeon, ed., *Introduction to Aristotle*, p. 313.

17. Christmas Humphreys, ed., *The Wisdom of Buddhism* (New York: Random House, 1961), pp. 65-66.

18. Humphreys, ed., *The Wisdom of Buddhism*, p. 50.

19. Humphreys, ed., *The Wisdom of Buddhism*, p. 90.

20. Humphreys, ed., *The Wisdom of Buddhism*, pp. 45-46.

21. Humphreys, ed., *The Wisdom of Buddhism*, p. 71.

22. Humphreys, ed., *The Wisdom of Buddhism*, p. 71.

23. Fritz Heider, *The Life of a Psychologist: An Autobiography* (Lawrence, Kansas: University Press of Kansas, 1983), p. 154.

24. Lin Yutang, ed., *The Wisdom of Confucius* (New York: Modern Library/Random House, 1938), p. 184.

25. Lin Yutang, ed., *The Wisdom of Confucius*, p. 280.

26. Mircea Eliade, *A History of Religious Ideas*, vol. 2, *From Gautama Buddha to the Triumph of Christianity*, tr. Willard R. Trask (Chicago: University of Chicago Press, 1982), p. 25.

27. Zengetsu, a Chinese Zen master of the T'ang dynasty, in Paul Reps, ed., *Zen Flesh, Zen Bones: A Collection of Zen and Pre-Zen Writings* (Garden City, N.Y.: Anchor/Doubleday, no date), p. 66.

Chapter 4

1. See, for example, Patrick H. Nowell-Smith, "Religion and Morality," in *The Encyclopedia of Philosophy*, vol. 7 (New York: Macmillan, 1967), pp. 150–158.

2. James Henry Breasted, *The Dawn of Conscience* (New York: Charles Scribner's Sons, 1934), pp. 125–126.

3. Breasted, *The Dawn of Conscience*, p. 256.

4. See S. H. Hooke, *Babylonian and Assyrian Religion* (Norman, Oklahoma: University of Oklahoma Press, 1963).

5. Breasted, *The Dawn of Conscience*, p. 341.

6. Deuteronomy, 15:7–8, Revised Standard Version.

7. Amos, 2:6–8.

8. Amos, 5:21–24.

9. Isaiah, 45:6–8.

10. Psalms, 19:7–10.

11. See J. Coert Rylaarsdam, *Revelation in Jewish Wisdom Literature* (Chicago: University of Chicago Press, 1946), pp. 66ff.

12. Job, 28:12–13.

13. See particularly Ecclesiasticus, 19:20, and chap. 24 passim.

14. The Wisdom of Solomon, 9:14.

15. The Wisdom of Solomon, 7:7, 9:1ff.

16. Francis Edwards Peters, *The Harvest of Hellenism: A History of the Near East from Alexander the Great to the Triumph of Christianity* (New York: Simon and Schuster, 1970), p. 445.

17. See Plato, Republic, book 7.

18. Job, 15:14.

19. Romans, 7:18.

20. Augustine, Confessions, in Augustine, *Basic Writings*, vol. 1 (New York: Random House, 1948), p. 25.

21. Augustine, Confessions, p. 24.

22. The philosopher Alasdair MacIntyre has recently drawn attention to the significance of this failure for the moral predicaments of our current culture. See *After Virtue: A Study in Moral Theory*, 2d ed. (Notre Dame, Indiana: University of Notre Dame Press, 1984). We will in the rest of this chapter, however, give a different interpretation from his of the reasons for this failure, leading to a different prognosis.

23. John Herman Randall, Jr., *The Making of the Modern Mind* (New York: Columbia University Press, 1976), p. 367.

24. See Baruch Spinoza, "Ethic," in Baruch Spinoza, *Selections* (New York: Charles Scribner's Sons, 1930).

25. David Hume, "An Enquiry Concerning the Principles of Morals," in David Hume, *Selections* (New York: Charles Scribner's Sons, 1927), p. 243. Emphasis Hume's.

26. Hume, "An Enquiry Concerning the Principles of Morals," p. 244.

27. Immanuel Kant, "Theory of Ethics," in Immanuel Kant, *Selections* (New York: Charles Scribner's Sons, 1929), p. 302.

28. See Kant, "Theory of Ethics," pp. 281ff.

29. See John Rawls, *A Theory of Justice* (Cambridge, Mass.: Harvard University Press, 1971).

30. See John Rawls, "Fairness to Goodness," *Philosophical Review*, 84 (1975), 536–554.

31. See Alan Gewirth, *Reason and Morality* (Chicago: University of Chicago Press, 1978).

32. Hume, "An Enquiry Concerning the Principles of Morals," pp. 215–216.

33. Joseph Butler, Sermon 3, in Lewis A. Selby-Bigge, ed., *British Moralists*, vol. 1 (Indianapolis: Bobbs-Merrill, 1964), p. 225.

34. See Kant, "Theory of Ethics," pp. 360ff.

35. See Kant, "Theory of Ethics," pp. 276–277.

36. Thomas Geoghegan, "Warren Court Children: The Angst of an Aging Activist," *The New Republic*, May 19, 1986, p. 23.

37. Augustine, "On the Grace of Christ and on Original Sin," in Augustine, *Basic Writings,* vol. 1 (New York: Random House, 1948), p. 616.

38. Blaise Pascal, "The Apology," in Blaise Pascal, *Pensées* (New York: Pantheon, 1965), p. 79.

39. Mencius is quoted in E. Royston Pike, *Ethics of the Great Religions* (London: Watts and Co., 1948), p. 227.

40. Peter Applebome, "Toddler is Rescued after 2-1/2 Days in Texas Well," *The New York Times,* Oct. 17, 1987, p. 1.

Chapter 5

1. The prevalence of this view is extensively documented in Michael A. Wallach and Lise Wallach, *Psychology's Sanction for Selfishness: The Error of Egoism in Theory and Therapy* (New York: W. H. Freeman and Co., 1983).

2. Sigmund Freud, "The Future of an Illusion," in James Strachey, ed., *The Standard Edition of the Complete Psychological Works of Sigmund Freud,* vol. 21 (London: Hogarth Press, 1961), p. 11.

3. Joan E. Sieber, "A Social Learning Theory Approach to Morality," in Myra Windmiller, Nadine Lambert, and Elliot Turiel, eds., *Moral Development and Socialization* (Boston: Allyn and Bacon, 1980), p. 138.

4. See, for example, Martin L. Hoffman, "Developmental Synthesis of Affect and Cognition and Its Implications for Altruistic Motivation," *Developmental Psychology,* 11 (1975), 607–622; Dale F. Hay and Harriet L. Rheingold, "The Early Appearance of Some Valued Social Behaviors," in Diane L. Bridgeman, ed., *The Nature of Prosocial Development* (New York: Academic Press, 1983); and Wallach and Wallach, *Psychology's Sanction for Selfishness.*

5. Hoffman, "Developmental Synthesis of Affect and Cognition and Its Implications for Altruistic Motivation," p. 614.

6. Judy Dunn and Carol Kendrick, *Siblings* (Cambridge, Mass.: Harvard University Press, 1982), p. 115.

7. Anna Freud and Dorothy Burlingham, *Infants without Families* (New York: International University Press, 1944), p. 40.

8. Hoffman, "Developmental Synthesis of Affect and Cognition and Its Implications for Altruistic Motivation," p. 615.

9. See Dunn and Kendrick, *Siblings*.

10. Dunn and Kendrick, *Siblings*, p. 98.

11. Lois Barclay Murphy, *Social Behavior and Child Personality* (New York: Columbia University Press, 1937), p. 297.

12. See E. Mark Cummings, Barbara Hollenbeck, Ronald Iannotti, Marian Radke-Yarrow, and Carolyn Zahn-Waxler, "Early Organization of Altruism and Aggression: Developmental Patterns and Individual Differences," in Carolyn Zahn-Waxler, E. Mark Cummings, and Ronald Iannotti, eds., *Altruism and Aggression: Biological and Social Origins* (Cambridge, England: Cambridge University Press, 1986).

13. See Abraham Sagi and Martin L. Hoffman, "Empathic Distress in the Newborn," *Developmental Psychology*, 12 (1976), 175–176; and Grace B. Martin and Russell D. Clark III, "Distress Crying in Neonates: Species and Peer Specificity," *Developmental Psychology*, 18 (1982), 3–9.

14. See Jeffrey F. Cohn and Edward Z. Tronick, "Three-Month-Old Infants' Reaction to Simulated Maternal Depression," *Child Development*, 54 (1983), 185–193.

15. See Carl J. Erickson, "Sexual Affiliation in Animals: Pair Bonds and Reproductive Strategies," in John B. Hutchison, ed., *Biological Determinants of Sexual Behavior* (New York: Wiley, 1978).

16. For these and other examples, see, for instance, Richard Dawkins, *The Selfish Gene* (New York: Oxford University Press, 1976), and Robert Trivers, *Social Evolution* (Menlo Park, Calif.: Benjamin/Cummings, 1985).

17. Dawkins, *The Selfish Gene*, p. 3. Emphasis Dawkins's.

18. David Barash, *The Whisperings Within* (New York: Harper and Row, 1979), p. 168. See also Donald T. Campbell, "On the Conflicts between Biological and Social Evolution and between Psychology and Moral Tradition," *American Psychologist*, 30 (1975), 1103–1126; Donald T. Campbell, "The Two Distinct Routes beyond Kin Selection to Ultrasociality: Implications for the Humanities and Social Sciences," in Bridgeman, ed., *The Nature of Prosocial Development*; and Edward O. Wilson, *On Human Nature* (Cambridge, Mass.: Harvard University Press, 1978).

19. Christopher R. Badcock, *The Problem of Altruism: Freudian-Darwinian Solutions*. (Oxford: Basil Blackwell, 1986), p. 18.

20. See, for example, Warren G. Holmes and Paul W. Sherman, "Kin Recognition in Animals," *American Scientist*, 71 (1983), 46–55.

21. See C. Daniel Batson, "Sociobiology and the Role of Religion in Promoting Prosocial Behavior: An Alternative View," *Journal of Personality and Social Psychology*, 45 (1983), 1380–1385; based on an account reported in the press.

22. See, for example, Dawkins, *The Selfish Gene;* Barash, *The Whisperings Within*; and Edward O. Wilson, *On Human Nature*.

23. See David Sloan Wilson, *The Natural Selection of Populations and Communities* (Menlo Park, Calif.: Benjamin/Cummings, 1980).

24. See W. Arens, *The Original Sin: Incest and Its Meaning* (New York: Oxford University Press, 1986), pp. 88ff.

25. See Arens, *The Original Sin*, pp. 80ff.

26. See Robert Axelrod and William D. Hamilton, "The Evolution of Cooperation," *Science*, 211 (1981), 1390–1396; and Robert Axelrod, *The Evolution of Cooperation* (New York: Basic Books, 1984).

27. Axelrod and Hamilton, "The Evolution of Cooperation."

28. Axelrod, *The Evolution of Cooperation*, p. ix.

29. Axelrod and Hamilton, "The Evolution of Cooperation," pp. 1394–1395.

30. Jean Jacques Rousseau, *Emile*, tr. Barbara Foxley (London: J. M. Dent and Sons, 1911), p. 5.

31. Harry Stack Sullivan, *The Interpersonal Theory of Psychiatry* (New York: W. W. Norton and Co., 1953), pp. 213–214.

32. See Karen Horney, *Neurosis and Human Growth: The Struggle toward Self-Realization* (New York: W. W. Norton and Co., 1950).

33. Eugene T. Gendlin, "Carl Rogers (1902–1987)," *American Psychologist*, 43 (1988), 127.

34. Carl R. Rogers, "Toward a Modern Approach to Values: The Valuing Process in the Mature Person," in Carl R. Rogers and Barry Stevens, eds., *Person to Person: The Problem of Being Human* (New York: Pocket Books, 1971), p. 15.

35. Abraham H. Maslow, *Motivation and Personality*, 2d ed. (New York: Harper and Row, 1970), p. 68.

36. Quoted in Frances FitzGerald, "A Reporter at Large: Rajneeshpuram," pt. 1, *The New Yorker*, Sept. 22, 1986, p. 82.

37. Richard Sennett, *Authority* (New York: Alfred A. Knopf, 1980), p. 130.

38. Edward C. Stewart, "American Assumptions and Values: Orientation to Action," in Elise C. Smith and Louise Fiber Luce, eds., *Toward Internationalism: Readings in Cross-Cultural Communication* (Rowley, Mass.: Newbury House Publishers, Inc., 1979), p. 2.

39. Philip L. Smith, "Still Hoping to Construct a Good Society: Dewey and Ethics," *Harvard Educational Review*, 56 (1986), 185.

40. Drew Westen, *Self and Society: Narcissism, Collectivism, and the Development of Morals* (Cambridge, England: Cambridge University Press, 1985), p. 345.

41. Kathleen Fisher, "Perloff: Self-Interest Getting Bad Rap," *American Psychological Association Monitor*, Oct. 1986, p. 8.

42. Lionel Trilling, *Sincerity and Authenticity* (Cambridge, Mass.: Harvard University Press, 1972), p. 64.

43. Oliver Sacks, *The Man Who Mistook His Wife for a Hat and Other Clinical Tales* (New York: Summit Books, 1985), p. 175.

44. Reynolds Price, *Kate Vaiden* (New York: Atheneum, 1986).

45. Robert Towers, "Ways Down South," *The New York Review of Books*, Sept. 25, 1986, p. 55.

46. Clifford Geertz, "Person, Time, and Conduct in Bali," in Clifford Geertz, *The Interpretation of Cultures* (New York: Basic Books, 1973), p. 379.

47. See Rodney Needham, "Inner States as Universals: Sceptical Reflections on Human Nature," in Paul Heelas and Andrew Lock, eds., *Indigenous Psychologies: The Anthropology of the Self* (London: Academic Press, 1981).

48. Clifford Geertz, "'From the Native's Point of View': On the Nature of Anthropological Understanding," in Richard A. Shweder and Robert A. LeVine, eds., *Culture Theory: Essays on Mind, Self, and Emotion* (Cambridge, England: Cambridge University Press, 1984), p. 129.

49. Judith N. Shklar, *Ordinary Vices* (Cambridge, Mass.: Harvard University Press, 1984), p. 73.

50. Shklar, *Ordinary Vices*, p. 74.

Chapter 6

1. Allan Bloom, *The Closing of the American Mind* (New York: Simon and Schuster, 1987).

2. Hans-Georg Gadamer, *Wahrheit und Methode: Grundzüge einer Philosophischen Hermeneutik* (Tübingen, West Germany: J.C.B. Mohr, 1960), p. 363; our translation.

3. James S. Fishkin, *Beyond Subjective Morality: Ethical Reasoning and Political Philosophy* (New Haven, Conn.: Yale University Press, 1984), p. 157.

4. Fishkin, *Beyond Subjective Morality*, p. 1.

5. Quoted from an interview in Fishkin, *Beyond Subjective Morality*, p. 37.

6. John Sabini and Maury Silver, *Moralities of Everyday Life* (New York: Oxford University Press, 1982), pp. 218–219.

7. Sabini and Silver, *Moralities of Everyday Life*, p. 204.

8. Richard J. Bernstein, *Beyond Objectivism and Relativism: Science, Hermeneutics, and Praxis* (Philadelphia: University of Pennsylvania Press, 1983), pp. 3–4.

9. See Thomas S. Kuhn, *The Structure of Scientific Revolutions*, 2d ed. (Chicago: University of Chicago Press, 1970).

10. Quoted in Thomas S. Kuhn, *The Copernican Revolution: Planetary Astronomy in the Development of Western Thought* (Cambridge, Mass.: Harvard University Press, 1957), p. 190.

11. Kuhn, *The Copernican Revolution*, p. 149.

12. Kuhn,*The Copernican Revolution*, p. 226.

13. Kuhn, *The Structure of Scientific Revolutions*, pp. 198–199. Emphasis Kuhn's.

14. See Alasdair MacIntyre, *After Virtue: A Study in Moral Theory*, 2d ed. (Notre Dame, Indiana: University of Notre Dame Press, 1984), pp. 19–20. MacIntyre's work has been enormously helpful to us, often serving as the point of departure for our own ideas.

15. See MacIntyre, *After Virtue*, Postscript to the Second Edition, and Alasdair MacIntyre, *Whose Justice? Which Rationality?* (Notre Dame, Indiana: University of Notre Dame Press, 1988).

16. MacIntyre, *After Virtue*, p. 276.

17. Richard Rorty, "Freud and Moral Reflection," in Joseph H. Smith and William Kerrigan, eds., *Pragmatism's Freud: The Moral Disposition of Psychoanalysis* (Baltimore: The Johns Hopkins University Press, 1986), p. 12.

18. Rorty, Freud and Moral Reflection, pp. 9–10.

19. See Kenneth J. Gergen, "The Social Constructionist Movement in Modern Psychology," *American Psychologist*, 40 (1985), 266–275.

20. See Barry Schwartz, *The Battle for Human Nature: Science, Morality, and Modern Life* (New York: W. W. Norton and Co., 1986).

21. Richard Rorty, *Contingency, Irony, and Solidarity* (Cambridge, England: Cambridge University Press, 1989), p. 177.

22. Alasdair MacIntyre, *A Short History of Ethics* (New York: Macmillan, 1966), p. 77.

23. See Colin M. Turnbull, *The Mountain People* (New York: Simon and Schuster, 1972).

24. Turnbull, *The Mountain People*, p. 289.

25. Turnbull, *The Mountain People*, p. 294.

26. Turnbull, *The Mountain People*, p. 227.

Chapter 7

1. See Margaret Adams, "The Compassion Trap," in Vivian Gornick and Barbara K. Moran, eds., *Woman in Sexist Society* (New York: New American Library, 1972).

2. Jean Bethke Elshtain, "Feminists Against the Family," *The Nation*, Nov. 17, 1979, p. 498. This is not Elshtain's own view, but her paraphrase of the position taken by some feminists.

3. See Sylvia Ann Hewlett, *A Lesser Life: The Myth of Women's Liberation in America* (New York: Warner Books, 1987).

4. Hewlett, *A Lesser Life*, p. 146.

5. Hewlett, *A Lesser Life*, p. 177.

6. See Carol Gilligan, *In a Different Voice: Psychological Theory and Women's Development* (Cambridge, Mass.: Harvard University Press, 1982).

7. Carol Gilligan, "Remapping Development: The Power of Divergent Data," in Leonard Cirillo and Seymour Wapner, eds., *Value Presuppositions in Theories of Human Development* (Hillsdale, N.J.: Lawrence Erlbaum Associates, 1986), p. 40.

8. Gilligan, "Remapping Development," p. 40.

9. Gilligan, *In a Different Voice*, p. 19.

10. Gilligan, *In a Different Voice*, p. 20.

11. See, for example, discussion following Gilligan's paper, "Remapping Development," in Cirillo and Wapner, eds., *Value Presuppositions in Theories of Human Development*, p. 59.

12. See, for example, Carol Gilligan, "Remapping the Moral Domain: New Images of the Self in Relationship," in Thomas C. Heller, Morton Sosna, and David E. Wellbery, eds., *Reconstructing Individualism: Autonomy, Individuality, and the Self in Western Thought* (Stanford, Calif.: Stanford University Press, 1986), p. 242; Gilligan, "Remapping Development," p. 40, and discussion following, p. 59; Carol Gilligan, "Moral Orientation and Moral Development," in Eva Feder Kittay and Diana T. Meyers, eds., *Women and Moral Theory* (Totowa, N.J.: Rowman and Littlefield, 1987), pp. 19, 30; and Carol Gilligan and Grant Wiggins, "The Origins of Morality in Early Childhood Relationships," in Jerome Kagan and Sharon Lamb, eds., *The Emergence of Morality in Young Children* (Chicago: University of Chicago Press, 1987), p. 283.

13. Cirillo and Wapner, eds., *Value Presuppositions in Theories of Human Development*.

14. Virginia Held, "Feminism and Moral Theory," in Kittay and Meyers, eds., *Women and Moral Theory*, p. 119.

15. See Thomas E. Hill, Jr., "The Importance of Autonomy," and Diana T. Meyers, "The Socialized Individual and Individual Autonomy," both in Kittay and Meyers, eds., *Women and Moral Theory*.

16. Gilligan, *In a Different Voice*, p. 99.

17. See Larry Blum, Marcia Homiak, Judy Housman, and Naomi Scheman, "Altruism and Women's Oppression," *The Philosophical Forum*, 5 (1973–1974), 222–247.

18. Benjamin R. Barber, *Strong Democracy: Participatory Politics for a New Age* (Berkeley, Calif.: University of California Press, 1984), p. 20.

19. William Sullivan, *Reconstructing Public Philosophy* (Berkeley, Calif.: University of California Press, 1982), p. 103.

20. Select Committee on Children, Youth, and Families, *Children, Youth, and Families: 1983* (Washington, D.C.: U.S. Government Printing Office, 1984), p. 103.

21. Select Committee on Children, Youth, and Families, *Families*

and Child Care: Improving the Options (Washington, D.C.: U.S. Government Printing Office, 1984), p. 23.

22. Michael H. K. Irwin, *Nuclear Energy: Good or Bad?* (New York: Public Affairs Pamphlets, 1984), p. 19.

23. Quoted in Robert L. Heilbroner, *An Inquiry into the Human Prospect: Updated and Reconsidered for the 1980's* (New York: W. W. Norton and Co., 1980), p. 180.

24. Marge Piercy, *Woman on the Edge of Time* (New York: Alfred A. Knopf, 1976), p. 232.

25. Sullivan, *Reconstructing Public Philosophy*, pp. 189–190.

26. Marcus G. Raskin, *The Common Good: Its Politics, Policies, and Philosophy* (New York: Routledge and Kegan Paul, 1986).

27. Robert N. Bellah, Richard Madsen, William M. Sullivan, Ann Swidler, and Steven M. Tipton, *Habits of the Heart: Individualism and Commitment in American Life* (Berkeley, Calif.: University of California Press, 1985).

28. Sullivan, *Reconstructing Public Philosophy*.

29. Michael J. Sandel, *Liberalism and the Limits of Justice* (Cambridge, England: Cambridge University Press, 1982).

30. Michael J. Sandel, ed., *Liberalism and Its Critics* (New York: New York University Press, 1984).

31. See, for example, Michael J. Sandel, Introduction, in Sandel, ed., *Liberalism and Its Critics*, p. 7.

32. See especially Sandel, *Liberalism and the Limits of Justice*, pp. 150, 161, and Introduction, pp. 5–6.

33. Paul R. Hanna, "Social Science," in *The World Book Encyclopedia*, (Chicago: World Book, Inc., 1986), p. 449.

34. Sidney B. Simon, "Values Clarification vs. Indoctrination," in David Purpel and Kevin Ryan, eds., *Moral Education: . . . It Comes with the Territory* (Berkeley, Calif.: McCutchan Publishing Corp., 1976), p. 135.

35. Anne Colby, Lawrence Kohlberg, and collaborators, *The Measurement of Moral Judgment*, vol. 1, *Theoretical Foundations and Research Validation* (Cambridge, England: Cambridge University Press, 1987), p. 20.

36. Lawrence Kohlberg, "The Cognitive-Developmental Approach to Moral Education," in Purpel and Ryan, eds., *Moral Education*, p. 183.

37. See, for example, Lawrence Kohlberg, *Essays on Moral Development*, vol. 1, *The Philosophy of Moral Development* (San Francisco: Harper and Row, 1981), p. 152.

38. Kohlberg, *Essays on Moral Development*, vol. 1, *The Philosophy of Moral Development*, p. 3.

39. Colby, Kohlberg, and collaborators, *The Measurement of Moral Judgment*, vol. 1, *Theoretical Foundations and Research Validation*, p. 20.

40. Lawrence Kohlberg, "The Just Community Approach to Moral Education in Theory and Practice," in Marvin W. Berkowitz and Fritz Oser, eds., *Moral Education: Theory and Application* (Hillsdale, N.J.: Lawrence Erlbaum Associates, 1985), p. 30.

41. See Lawrence Kohlberg, "Revisions in the Theory and Practice of Moral Development," in William Damon, ed., *Moral Development: New Directions for Child Development*, no. 2 (San Francisco: Jossey-Bass, 1978), pp. 84–85.

42. Lawrence Kohlberg, "High School Democracy and Educating for a Just Society," in Ralph L. Mosher, ed., *Moral Education: A First Generation of Research and Development* (New York: Praeger, 1980), p. 28. See also Kohlberg, "The Just Community Approach to Moral Education in Theory and Practice," in Berkowitz and Oser, eds., *Moral Education*.

43. See, for example, Kohlberg, "High School Democracy and Educating for a Just Society," in Mosher, ed., *Moral Education*, p. 49.

44. See especially Lawrence Kohlberg, *Essays on Moral Development*, vol. 2, *The Psychology of Moral Development* (San Francisco: Harper and Row, 1984); and Colby, Kohlberg, and collaborators, *The Measurement of Moral Judgment*, vol. 1, *Theoretical Foundations and Research Validation*.

45. Kohlberg, *Essays on Moral Development*, vol. 1, *The Philosophy of Moral Development*, p. 351.

INDEX

Adkins, A. W. H., 42
Agathos, 41–43
"Agents of socialization." *See* Socialization
Altruism, genetics and. *See* Biology, evolutionary
Amos, 56
Architecture, posturing in, 5–6
Arete, 41–44
Aristotle, 40–41, 43–47, 49, 51–54, 59, 63–66, 68, 70–71, 84, 88, 107, 112, 114, 123
Augustine, 59
Axelrod, Robert, 80–83

Balinese, 92–93
Ballard, Michael, 5
Barber, Benjamin R., 124
Behaviorism, 52, 69–70, 72–73, 84–85, 89
Bellah, Robert N., vii, 6–7, 125
Berger, Peter, 4
Berlin, Isaiah, 1
Bernstein, Richard J., 105
Biology, evolutionary, 71–84, 127–128, 132–133
Bloom, Allan, vii–viii, 7, 101
Bodin, Jean, 106–107, 111
Book of the Dead, 55
Buddha, 40, 48–52, 54, 65, 68, 112, 114
Butler, Joseph, 64

Callicles, 43–44, 48, 63
Career counseling, 2–3
Categorical imperative, 62
Character education, 9, 128
Children: care of, 119–120, 124, 128; observations of, 73–74, 127
Christ, 40, 55, 57, 59
Civic republicanism, viii, 125
Clarke, Samuel, 61

INDEX

Clustering, 82–83
Communitarianism, 124–128
Confucius, 40, 48, 50–52, 54, 65–66, 68, 112, 114
Conscience: Butler on, 64; internalization and, 9–10, 48, 54, 60–61, 69–70, 85
Consciousness raising, 14, 52, 71, 114, 132
Conventional moral level, 129–131
Copernicus, 106–107

Dance, posturing in, 5–6
Darwin, Charles, 75
Democracy, 125–126
Dewey, John, 129
Dikaiosune, 42
Dispersal with maturity. *See* Out-breeding

Ecology, 124–125, 128
Economics, 4, 75, 119, 124
Elshtain, Jean Bethke, 146n.2
Ethnocentrism, 109
Etzioni, Amitai, 4
Eudaimonia, 45–46
Euripides, 42, 137n.6
Evolution. *See* Biology, evolutionary

Feminism, 118–123, 132
Figure-ground analogy, 120, 123
Fishkin, James S., 103–104, 106, 108–109
"Forms," Platonic, 44, 58
Franklin, Benjamin, 94
Free riders, 77–83, 127
Freud, Sigmund, 3, 47, 52, 69–70, 72, 75, 84–87, 89, 124, 131
Friendship, nature of, 123

Gadamer, Hans-Georg, 102
Gadamerian conversation, 102–103, 112, 115, 123, 132
Geertz, Clifford, 92–93
Generational series, 21, 91–92
Genes. *See* Biology, evolutionary
Geocentric vs. heliocentric theories, 106–107, 111
Gewirth, Alan, 63
Gilligan, Carol, vii–viii, 8, 120–123, 132
Goldhill, Simon, 137n.6
"Good errors," 102
Gould, Glenn, 93

Group traditions. *See* Traditions

Hamilton, William D., 80, 82–83
Hammurabi, 55
Handel, George Frederick, 93
Harkuf of Elephantine, 55
Hauerwas, Stanley, 7
Heider, Fritz, 50
Heliocentric vs. geocentric theories, 106–107, 111
Heroic models, 132
Hesiod, 41
Hewlett, Sylvia Ann, 119
Hitler, Adolf, 126
Hobbes, Thomas, 124
Homer, 40–41, 44
Horney, Karen, 85
Humanism: criticisms of, 70–72, 84–94, 102–103; modern forms of, vii, ix, 45–46, 51–52
Hume, David, 61–64, 66, 73, 112, 121
Huxtable, Ada Louise, 5–6

"Ideas," Platonic, 44, 58
Ik, 113–115, 127
Ilongot, 110
Individualism: cultural responses to, vii–viii, 5–8, 125; social science supports of, 2–4, 129–132
Indoctrination, 128–132
Internalization: communitarian goals and, 125, 127; criticism of concept of, 9–10, 54, 60–61; psychological discussions of, 69–70, 72–74, 85–86, 130
Introspective psychology, 93
Isaiah, second, 56

Jesus. *See* Christ
Job, 57, 59
"Just communities," 131
Justification in ethics vs. science, 103–115. *See also* Relativism

Kagan, Jerome, 7
Kant, Immanuel, 62–65
Kohlberg, Lawrence, 128–132
Kohut, Heinz, 3, 84
Kuhn, Thomas S., 105, 108, 110

!Kung, 109

"Lek," 93
Locke, John, 124
Loevinger, Jane, 3
Luther, Martin, 59

MacIntyre, Alasdair, vii, 109–110, 112–113, 140n.22, 145n.14
Maslow, Abraham H., 52, 85–86
Mencius, 51, 66
Moral developmentalism, 129–132
Moral education, 128–132
Moses, 56
Mozart, Wolfgang Amadeus, 93
Mystery religions, 58

Narcissism, vii–ix, 6–7. See also Individualism
National Organization for Women, 119
Natural selection. See Biology, evolutionary
Neo-Freudians, 52, 70, 84–85
Newton, Isaac, 60
Nietzsche, Friedrich W., 43, 48, 63
Nozick, Robert, 124

Objectivity in ethics, 95–115, 129
"Orthodox" Confucian tradition, 51, 66
Out-breeding, 78–80, 83, 127

Pascal, Blaise, 66
Paul, 59
Percy, Walker, 12
Piercy, Marge, 125
Plato, 40–41, 43–47, 49, 51–54, 58–59, 63–66, 68, 70–71, 84, 88, 112, 114
Politics, 124–128
Postconventional moral level, 130–132
Postmodernism: in architecture, 5–6; in Western thought, 105–106, 117
Preconventional moral level, 129, 131
Price, Reynolds, 91
"Prisoner's dilemma," 80–83
Psychoanalysis. See Freud, Sigmund; Kohut, Heinz; Neo-Freudians
Psychological humanism. See Humanism
Psychology: knowledge of own motives in, 47, 49; self-orientation in, 3–4, 6, 69–72, 102–103; spontaneity in, 13, 52–54, 84–94, 129

Raskin, Marcus G., 125

Rawls, John, 63, 104
Reciprocal cooperation, 80–83, 127
Reincarnation, doctrine of, 50
Relativism, 95–115, 128–130
Rogers, Carl R., 3, 13, 52, 85–86, 89, 129
Roles, 3–5, 12, 90–94, 113, 118
Rorty, Richard, 112–113
Roth, Philip, 2
Rousseau, Jean Jacques, 13, 70, 84–85, 90–91

Sabini, John, 104–106, 108–109
Sacks, Oliver, 91
Sandel, Michael J., 125
Schwartz, Barry, 112–113
Secular humanism. *See* Humanism
Self-actualization, 85–87, 117–118
Self-realization, 85
Sennett, Richard, 88
"Shaping," 91. *See also* Behaviorism; Socialization
Shklar, Judith N., 94
"Shoulds," 14, 85, 88–89
Silver, Maury, 104–106, 108–109
Singer, Peter, 104
Sirach, 57
Social constructionism, 112–113
Social contract, 62–63, 124–125
Socialization: communitarian goals and, 125–126, 128; criticism of concept of, ix, 9–10, 54, 60–61; psychological discussions of, 29, 69–70, 72–73, 112–113, 129–130
Social learning theory, 52, 69–70, 72–73, 89, 129–131
Socrates, 44–46, 49
Solomon, 57
Sophists, 43
Spinoza, Baruch, 61
Subjectivism, 95–115
Sullivan, Harry Stack, 85
Sullivan, William M., 124–125

Terrorism, apologetics for, 100
Theognis, 42
Therapeutic attitude, 102–103, 115
Therapy. *See* Psychology
"Tit for tat." *See* Reciprocal cooperation
Traditions, viii, 104–114, 125–128
Trilling, Lionel, 91

Turnbull, Colin M., 113–114

Utilitarianism, 64, 104

Values clarification, 129–130, 132
Valuing reaction, 89, 102, 109
"Virtues, bag of," 128

Wilson, David Sloan, 78–80, 127

Zengetsu, 139n.27